T0305916

"In *Public Relations and Sustainable Citizenship*, Munshi and Kurian once again deliver a powerful work of the highest quality scholarship that insists on our attention. Shifting the terrain for both functional and critical approaches to public relations, they emphasise the fundamental importance of action, connection and relationship to resistance communication. As a way of understanding the many acts of resistance to planetary domination by capitalist and political elites, the power of public relations for sustainable citizenship is both emergent, built on organic connections that grow as causes and concerns multiply, and urgent, built on a passion for justice that should engage us all. As such, this book is not only a powerful alternative theorisation of public relations in the interests of the planet and its people; it is also a call to action for scholars and practitioners to democratise public relations and use its power productively."

– **Lee Edwards,** *London School of Economics and Political Science*

Public Relations and Sustainable Citizenship

This book examines how public relations might re-imagine itself as an instrument of "sustainable citizenship" by exploring alternative models of representing and building relationships with and among marginalized publics that disrupt the standard discourses of public relations. It argues that public relations needs to situate itself in the larger context of citizenship, the values and ethics that inform it, and the attitudes and behaviours that characterize it.

Interlacing critical public relations with a theoretical fabric woven with strands of postcolonial histories, Indigenous studies, feminist studies, and political theory, the book brings out the often-unseen processes of relationship building that nurture solidarity among historically marginalized publics. The book is illustrated with global cases of public relations as sustainable citizenship in action across three core elements of the earth: air, water, and land. In each of the cases, readers can see how resistance movements, not necessarily aligned with any specific organization or interest group, are seeking to change the status quo of a world increasingly defined by exploitation, overconsumption, sectarianism, and faux nationalism.

This challenging book will be of interest to students and scholars of not only public relations but also the broader social and management sciences who are committed to issues of environmental and social justice.

Debashish Munshi is Professor of Management Communication at the University of Waikato, New Zealand. His research interests lie at the intersections of communication, diversity, sustainability, social change, and citizenship. He is co-author of *Reconfiguring Public Relations: Ecology, Equity, and Enterprise* (2007) and co-editor of the *Handbook of Communication Ethics* (2011), *On the Edges of Development: Cultural Interventions* (2009), and *Feminist Futures: Re-imagining Women, Culture, and Development* (2016).

Priya Kurian is Professor of Political Science and Public Policy at the University of Waikato, New Zealand. Her research is interdisciplinary and involves work on environmental, social, and cultural sustainability through a focus on environmental politics and policy, science and technology studies, and development studies. She is the author of *Engendering the Environment? Gender in the World Bank's Environmental Policies* (2000) and co-editor of *Feminist Futures: Re-imagining Women, Culture, and Development* (2003; 2016), *On the Edges of Development: Cultural Interventions* (2009), and *International Organisations and Environmental Policy* (1995).

Routledge Insights in Public Relations Research

The field of PR research has grown exponentially in recent years and academics at all career levels are seeking authoritative publication opportunities for their scholarship. **Routledge Insights in Public Relations Research** is a new program of short-form book publications, presenting key topics across the discipline and their foundation in research. This series will provide a forward-facing global forum for new and emerging research topics which critically evaluate contemporary PR thinking and practice.

This format is particularly effective for introducing new scholarship reflecting the diverse range of research approaches and topics in the field. It is particularly effective for:

- Overview of an emerging area or "hot topic."
- In-depth case-study.
- Tailored research-based information for a practitioner readership.
- Update of a research paper to reflect new findings or wider perspectives.
- Exploration of analytical or theoretical innovations.
- Topical response to current affairs or policy debates.

Authors from practice and the academy will be able to quickly pass on their thinking and findings to fellow PR scholars, researchers, MA and PhD students and informed practitioners.

Public Relations as Public Diplomacy
The Royal Bank of Canada's Monthly Letter, 1943–2003
Sandra L. Braun

Public Relations and Sustainable Citizenship
Representing the Unrepresented
Debashish Munshi and Priya Kurian

For more information about this series, please visit: www.routledge.com/Routledge-Insights-in-Public-Relations-Research/book-series/RIPRR

Public Relations and Sustainable Citizenship

Representing the Unrepresented

**Debashish Munshi
and Priya Kurian**

Routledge
Taylor & Francis Group

LONDON AND NEW YORK

First published 2021
by Routledge
2 Park Square, Milton Park, Abingdon, Oxon OX14 4RN

and by Routledge
52 Vanderbilt Avenue, New York, NY 10017

Routledge is an imprint of the Taylor & Francis Group, an informa business

© 2021 Debashish Munshi and Priya Kurian

The right of Debashish Munshi and Priya Kurian to be identified as
authors of this work has been asserted by them in accordance with
sections 77 and 78 of the Copyright, Designs and Patents Act 1988.

All rights reserved. No part of this book may be reprinted or
reproduced or utilised in any form or by any electronic, mechanical,
or other means, now known or hereafter invented, including
photocopying and recording, or in any information storage or
retrieval system, without permission in writing from the publishers.

Trademark notice: Product or corporate names may be trademarks
or registered trademarks, and are used only for identification and
explanation without intent to infringe.

British Library Cataloguing-in-Publication Data
A catalogue record for this book is available from the British Library

Library of Congress Cataloging-in-Publication Data
Names: Munshi, Debashish, author. | Kurian, Priya A., author.
Title: Public relations and sustainable citizenship : representing the
    unrepresented / Debashish Munshi and Priya Kurian.
Description: New York : Routledge, 2020. | Includes bibliographical
    references and index.
Identifiers: LCCN 2020025693 (print) | LCCN 2020025694 (ebook) |
    ISBN 9780367338107 (hardback) | ISBN 9780429322044
    (ebook)
Subjects: LCSH: Public relations. | Communication—Moral and
    ethical aspects. | Social change.
Classification: LCC HM1221 .M86 2020 (print) | LCC HM1221
    (ebook) | DDC 659.2—dc23
LC record available at https://lccn.loc.gov/2020025693
LC ebook record available at https://lccn.loc.gov/2020025694

ISBN: 978-0-367-33810-7 (hbk)
ISBN: 978-0-429-32204-4 (ebk)

Typeset in Times New Roman
by Apex CoVantage, LLC

Contents

Acknowledgements

The seeds for this book were sown in a chapter (Munshi & Kurian, 2016) we wrote for *The Routledge Handbook of Critical Public Relations* edited by Jacquie L'Etang, David McKie, Nancy Snow, and Jordi Xifra (2016). We are grateful to Routledge, especially Jacqueline Curthoys and Kevin Moloney, for encouraging us to develop a book proposal, picking up on the ideas presented in the chapter in the *Handbook*. It has been a pleasure to work with Routledge. We thank in particular Guy Loft, Matthew Ranscombe and Grant Schatzman for staying in touch through the writing of the book.

We acknowledge the support of our home institution, the University of Waikato, especially the Waikato Management School and the Division of Arts, Law, Psychology, and Social Sciences, for giving us the time, space, and resources to work on the project. We also thank our second temporary home institution, the London School of Economics and Political Science, where we were both Visiting Senior Fellows in 2020, when a significant portion of the manuscript was written.

This book is a narrative that weaves together ideas gathered not only from reading scholarly works spanning several disciplines and following current affairs on international media but also from many conversations we have had with each other and with fellow researchers, activists, friends, and sometimes even strangers at public meetings. It is obviously impossible to acknowledge the contribution of every individual, but we would like to mention a few with whom we have had the most meaningful and stimulating conversations. These include research collaborators, co-authors, and co-conversationalists, including Patrick Barrett, Robert V. Bartlett, Kum-Kum Bhavnani, Kirsten Broadfoot, George Cheney, Raven Cretney, Radha D'Souza, John Foran, Lyn Kathlene, David McKie, Sandy Morrison, Anjali Prabhu, Rachel Simon-Kumar, Megan Smith, and Margalit Toledano, to name just a few. An extra special thank you goes out to Lee Edwards whose enthusiastic engagement with our work as well as incisive, insightful, and challenging comments have greatly enhanced the book. We thank our extended families, friends, and current and former students who have been active interlocutors on questions of sustainability, activism, and environmental and social justice. While so many people have contributed to whatever is valuable with the book, we alone are responsible for any drawbacks or errors in judgement. Finally, we share our appreciation for our research assistants, Malcolm Doo and Shaaliny Jaufar.

Some scattered segments of the book were part of a chapter in *The Routledge Handbook of Critical Public Relations* (Munshi & Kurian, 2016), and parts of Chapter 2 were presented as a keynote address at the European Communication Research and Education Association (ECREA) conference on "Complexity, hybridity, liminality: Challenges of researching contemporary promotional cultures" at the London School of Economics and Political Science on 21 February 2020 (Munshi & Kurian, 2020).

This book is dedicated to two young sustainable citizens, Akanksha and Alya, their cousins, friends, and all other young people working for and building communication frameworks for social and environmental justice around the world.

1   Theorizing public relations and sustainable citizenship

Is the 'public' in public relations really public? In taking a critical look at the discourses of public relations, we have consistently found a hierarchy of publics ranging from dominant elite publics that are relentlessly promoted to many who are not represented at all (Munshi & Kurian, 2005, 2007). If indeed, as we argue, public relations does not engage with a multitude of publics, or represent the unrepresented, can it ever play a role in grappling with the pressing issues facing global citizenry around the air we breathe, the water we imbibe, and the land on which we live? Each of the immediate issues affecting the wellbeing of the planet and its people revolves around seemingly intractable socio-political conflicts arising out of unequal dynamics of power. This has been particularly evident most recently in the huge gaps between the experiences of well-paid executives and poor migrant workers, the wealthy and the vulnerable, the healthy and those with underlying medical conditions, during the spread of the deadly novel coronavirus, COVID-19, alongside the national lockdowns to control the proliferation of the virus.

To truly live up to the 'public' in its name, public relations needs to situate itself "in the larger context of citizenship, the values and ethics that inform it and the attitudes and behaviours that characterize it" (Munshi & Kurian, 2016, p. 405). In this book, we look at how public relations might re-imagine itself as the practice of not merely citizenship but of what we call "sustainable citizenship" (Kurian, Munshi, & Bartlett, 2014; Munshi & Kurian, 2015). To do so, we first interrogate current conceptions of public relations and envision an alternative conceptual trajectory for it.

Re-imagining public relations

Constituting a relatively small sub-set of communication scholarship, the academic field of public relations has adopted many different approaches and has been conceived in a variety of ways. These include the pursuit of public relations of functional organizational goals articulated in, for example, 'Excellence Theory' (Grunig, 1992; Grunig, Grunig, & Dozier, 2002) and the 'Comparative Excellence Framework' (Vercic & Zerfass, 2016). These views live up to Grunig and Hunt's (1984) widely cited characterization of public relations as the "*management* of communication between an organization and its publics" (p. 6, emphasis added) and Cutlip, Center, and Broom's (2000) focus on only those publics on whom an organization's "success or failure depends" (p. 6). Much of the organization-centred public relations revolves around corporate interests, including building a corporation's reputation and minimizing risk to this reputation (Hutton, Goodman, Alexander, & Genest, 2001; Bailey, 2018) by lobbying government and other policy-making agencies, facilitating stories in the mass media and social media, managing crisis situations, building community relations, and promoting corporate social responsibility. At the other end of the spectrum is a view of public relations that challenges its functional attributes (Heath, Toth, & Waymer, 2009; Leitch & Motion, 2010) and theorizes public relations as a rhetorical and discursive device rather than merely a managerial function. The rhetorical approach sees public relations as symbolic and open to many different interpretations, thereby potentially allowing opportunities for organizations to co-construct meanings with their stakeholders (e.g., Heath, 2001, 2005; Ihlen & Heath, 2018; Ihlen, 2008). However, the centrality of message producers is evident in both functional and non-functional approaches to public relations with an actor or a collective of actors furthering specific interests through a series of messages and relationship-building exercises. As Moloney and McGrath (2020) observe, public relations

> is weak propaganda; it is persuasive communication for competitive advantage. This is as true when PR is undertaken by a cancer charity as it is when PR is employed by a global technology company. Public relations is fundamentally about the rhetorical expression of a private self-interest, but it takes place in public life. . . . Public relations is advocacy and counter-advocacy; it is adversarial rather than communitarian; it is argumentative rather than consensual; it seeks to create influence for its producers.
>
> (p. 148)

This reading of public relations as it is largely played out is very astute. Moloney and McGrath (2020) expose the pretence of public relations about its self-proclaimed attributes such as "mutual understanding, strategic communication, relationships and reputation management" (p. 148). They argue that the fact that public relations has a poor public image generally and is seen by the wider public as mere 'spin' is evidence of how far removed it is from either developing trust or conducting two-way symmetrical communication as several scholars and practitioners would have us believe (Moloney & McGrath, 2020).

Critical public relations, which has made rapid advances in recent years, has systematically interrogated public relations' lopsided power equations (see, e.g., Bardhan & Weaver, 2011; Curtin & Gaither, 2007; Demetrious, 2013; Dutta & Pal, 2010; Edwards, 2014); discussed its ethical deficit (Toledano, 2018); and outlined its insistence on furthering the interests of some publics over others (Munshi & Kurian, 2005). This area of scholarship has been on a continuing path of what McKie and Munshi (2007) call "reconfiguring public relations" to orient critical public relations towards improving the understanding of public relations "through more open approaches" that are not agenda-driven (L'Etang, 2005, p. 523) and are rooted in a variety of contexts, including economic, social, cultural, environmental, local, and global ones.

The diversity of approaches, as Edwards (2011) says, needs to be understood as "positions on a series of continua that address different ontological characteristics of PR" (p. 20). She outlines six "paradigmatic assumptions that underpin the scholarly approaches currently found in PR" (Edwards, 2011, p. 14). The functional ones of these are that the organizational context is very important; that "effective PR equates to 'well-managed' communications" that take care of an organization's interests and reputation; and that publics are defined in relation to the "organization's strategic communications interests" (Edwards, 2011, pp. 14–16). The non-functional assumptions are that public relations is not just about the organizational context; that it "is shaped by the cultures and societies in which it operates"; and that "it has the potential to engender both power and resistance" (Edwards, 2011, pp. 16–19). In essence, whether functional or non-functional, public relations is largely seen to be about individual or collective actors building relationships to further their own individual, organizational, or social group interests or resist the interests of others they see as adversarial.

It is in acknowledging the resistance of actors to dominant interests that activism is increasingly seen as a form of public relations (e.g., Coombs & Holladay, 2012; Curtin, 2016; Demetrious, 2013; Holtzhausen, 2014; Sommerfeldt, Kent, & Taylor, 2012; Toledano, 2016). Public relations has had, as L'Etang (2016) says, "a complicated relationship with activism because historically activism justified organisational investment in PR services and personnel" (p. 207), with activists seen by corporate managers in oppositional terms. Indeed, three decades ago, Grunig (1989) suggested that "activist groups create conflict between organizations and their environments," which, in turn, "creates the need for public relations" (p. 4). Since then, as more pluralistic views of public relations have evolved, activism has been described as "modern public relations" with an effort to unearth the "generally unseen contributions of activists to the development of public relations" (Coombs & Holladay, 2014, p. 63); indeed Moloney and McKie (2016) have even noted an "activist turn" in public relations (p. 154). Activism as public relations itself has many layers. These range from Berger and Reber's (2005) positioning of activism within organizational contexts, where public relations professionals work within corporate institutions to make sure such institutions are guided by ethics and public good, to Adi and Moloney's (2012) conception of "protest PR," which persuades policymakers "via occupations, demonstrations, strikes, public speaking, and other forms of non-violent and violent protest" (cited in Adi, 2019, p. 4) to bring about changes in legal and regulatory frameworks for policy change.

We acknowledge the work of activists and scholars in framing resistance as part of the ethical repertoire of public relations practices. However, unlike both functional and non-functional approaches to public relations, we take the emphasis away from *actors* who strategically deploy communication to manage their own interests or resist others' interests. Instead, we focus on the *action/s* of resistance that spark the organic emergence of alliances among publics fighting for justice and equity as public relations. In this sense, we look beyond public relations as "discourse technology" (Motion & Letich, 1996, 2016) in which "public relations practitioners are . . . discourse technologists who play a central role in the maintenance and transformation of discourse" (Motion & Letich, 1996, p. 298). By moving away from trying to find the *source* of public relations discourse – the actor or technologist representing an organization or an activist group – we shift our attention to the enactment of resistance and the discourses that emerge when unrepresented publics make their voices heard. This is not to say that actors are not important – they obviously are, but relationship building is not just about actors looking to centre their own interests in building strategic alliances with some publics and shunning others. In particular, the building of discourses of resistance by alliances and networks that attempt to challenge the exercise of unjust power by elite, dominant publics (often elite, dominant actors) is what we call *public relations as sustainable citizenship*. This insurgent form of public relations communicates the representation of the unrepresented.

Our focus on action as the embodiment of the collective pursuit of creating space in the public sphere is illuminated by the light refracted through three lenses of political thought: Historian Ranajit Guha's (1983) representation of the colonial history of India by writing about the acts of resistance of peasants who, though invisible in history, were by no means passive onlookers; Indigenous education scholar Linda Tuhiwai Smith's (1999/2012) re-orientation of research to be able to tell the counter stories of resistance of colonized Indigenous communities; and philosopher Hannah Arendt's (1958) assertion that actions of resistance have intrinsic worth – they are not merely a means to an end but also an end in themselves. In other words, the means themselves are an expression of the power of resistance. We blend the rays of these thoughts with our own work in *Feminist Futures* (Bhavnani, Foran, Kurian, & Munshi, 2016) in which we draw attention to the "movements of determined resistance" (p. xxii), often led by women in conjunction with Indigenous communities and other historically marginalized publics:

> Indeed, global and grassroots resistance movements that deeply comprehend women and gender inequalities and discourses remain humanity's best hope for a future that is inclusive, diverse, just, equitable and democratic, one that is based on a recognition of the dignity of all lives, human and non-human.
>
> (p. xxii)

Addressing imbalances of power has been the locus of study for subaltern historiographers such as Guha (1982, 1983). And there are lessons in their approaches for any project on re-conceptualizing public relations. Just as mainstream public relations tends to be equated with representing elite message producers and helping them build relationships with publics that matter to them, mainstream history presents a record of epochal events through the eyes of elites. Guha and his fellow South Asian historians have sought to decolonize history by compiling an impressive and influential collection of historical accounts from the perspective of the 'subaltern,' a term first used by Antonio Gramsci (1971) to denote groups subjected to the hegemony of the ruling classes. By looking at history through the eyes of the subaltern, these historians challenge the dominant histories written from the point of view of the colonizing elites. Guha (1983), for example, documented the resistance of peasant communities and the solidarity such resistance generated among publics ignored by the ruling classes.

If Guha and other subaltern historians make space for the representation of publics of whom elite histories had kept no record, Smith's (2012) *Decolonizing Methodologies* shows how mainstream research's "pursuit of knowledge is deeply embedded in the multiple layers of imperial and colonial practices" (p. 2), suppressing Indigenous thoughts and experiences. To counter this, Smith (2012) sets out to develop Indigenous methodologies for research that resist intrinsically imperialist ideas and create the space for Indigenous ways of thinking. She talks about Kaupapa Māori methodologies, for example, as "setting new directions for the priorities, policies, and practices of research for, by and with Māori" (Smith, 2012, p. 185). In essence, alternative pathways to research, too, are about addressing issues of power.

For subaltern communities, the actions of resistance they take tell a powerful story. In adapting the ideas of Arendt (1958, 1970, 1972), we see the source of the story or the material objectives of the story as less important than the message of the action undertaken. Looking at public relations through an Arendtian lens means that communicative action need not have an instrumental goal – the action itself could be the message. From such a perspective, any action that resists oppression, coercion, manipulation, or injustice and gives voice to structurally or discursively marginalized publics is an expression of a public relations that engages with the ideas of power, politics, and solidarity.

For Arendt (1972), power is different from strength, force, or violence, each of which is unleashed by dominant actors on marginalized publics. As d'Entreves (2019) explains, Arendt's view of power is that

> unlike strength, [it] is not the property of an individual, but of a plurality of actors joining together for some common political purpose. Unlike force, it is not a natural phenomenon but a human creation, the outcome of collective engagement. And unlike violence, it is based not on coercion but on consent and rational persuasion.

Power thus understood is the defining characteristic of society. Arendt's notion of power as the capacity to act with others and her focus on the community and the collective resonates with feminist notions of empowerment, that is, ideas of 'power to' rather than what are seen as more masculine conceptions of 'power over' (see, e.g., Hartsock, 1983; Allen, 2016). Like Arendt, and following Foucault (1980), Young (1990) calls for a relational notion of power, stating that "power exists only in action" (p. 32). Solidarity emerges from such an idea of power as an expression of acting in concert with others to resist forms of injustice. Solidarity is in fact an expression of the collective power of oppositional movements and seeks "to resist and transform deeply entrenched relations of dominance and subordination" (Allen, 1999, p. 112). As Fraser (1986) comments in the context of the potential for women's solidarity in an inclusive feminist movement, solidarity must be achieved politically; it "is never simply given" (p. 429). An example of the solidarity of the resistance movements itself translating into a solidarity among those writing about such movements is in the way the South Asian subaltern historians built an academic solidarity with their Latin American colleagues who, as Beverley (1994) says, have also been "writing in reverse" (p. 271). Acknowledging the solidarity of the Latin American scholars, Guha (2001) notes that "it is gestures like this, more than anything else, [that] make it possible for us to break out of containment in two hundred years of solitude" (p. 35).

The frame of power, politics, and solidarity is what we build our alternative idea of public relations as a form of communicative action on, which involves persuasion for social change (see, e.g., Dutta, 2011). Such action, for Arendt, arises

> out of the concerted activities of a plurality of agents, and it rests on persuasion because it consists in the ability to secure the consent of others through unconstrained discussion and debate. . . . It is actualized in all those cases where action is undertaken for communicative (rather than strategic or instrumental) purposes, and where speech is employed to disclose our intentions and to articulate our motives to others.
>
> (d'Entreves, 2019)

This alternative conceptualization of public relations endorses Moloney and McGrath's (2020) assertion that public relations "is existentially about persuasive communication" (p. 5), although, as they say, this aspect has been downplayed by scholars and practitioners alike. However, in focusing on communicative action intrinsically as an expression of the desire for social justice, we see public relations as a potential vehicle of power that resists dominant discourses regardless of whether it achieves any specific material goals. Fostering resistance disrupts hegemonic and hierarchical discourses of public relations and makes space in the public sphere for marginalized publics seeking justice. Rather than being limited to advancing the interests of specific organizations or groups, public relations as sustainable citizenship works (or can work) instead on facilitating advocacy for social, political, and environmental justice and transformative change (e.g., Dutta, 2011; L'Etang, 2016). In this book, we focus on social, environmental, and political campaigns for justice in resisting climate change, claiming water rights, and regaining dispossessed land. Each of these campaigns, built on radical communicative actions resisting a dominant narrative that has long held sway, embodies the notion of sustainable citizenship discussed next.

Sustainable citizenship and empowering publics

As both a concept and a process, sustainable citizenship "is an idea of active citizenship with an ethical commitment to long-term holistic sustainability grounded in social justice that explicitly recognises and addresses power differentials and marginality" (Munshi & Kurian, 2015). At its core, the notion of sustainable citizenship not only invokes but also re-imagines the two key ideas of sustainability and citizenship. While sustainability spans the three widely known dimensions of environment, society, and economy, grounded as it is in the need to protect the natural and material resources for the welfare of current and future generations, we point to a fourth dimension that is not talked about as much – the political dimension (Munshi & Kurian, 2015). It is in relation to political systems of structural domination that power is exercised and enacted, and it is power that ultimately shapes how decisions are made, resources are distributed, and injustice is challenged.

The idea of power is critical in protecting sustainability from being appropriated by elite publics that mainstream public relations has long chosen to service. The alliterative phrase, "People, Planet, and Profit" (Elkington, 1994), reflecting the triple bottom line (social, environmental, and financial) of sustainability, has indeed been a rhetorical mask for several corporations trying to gloss over their many unsustainable practices. As we document in Chapter 2, corporations have used the strength of their abundant financial resources to massage the interests of capitalist, shareholding publics at the expense of the many diverse publics that make up the democratic realm.

Like sustainability, the idea of citizenship needs to be re-imagined in the changing contexts of modern societies by factoring in the dynamics of power. These contexts have become increasingly complex with confrontations between capitalist globalization and grassroots activism as well as the rapidly changing role of the state in maintaining democratic processes (Kurian et al., 2014, p. 438). We argue that citizenship in democratic contexts can deliver for the people and the planet if it acknowledges and addresses economic, social, structural, and political causes of inequality and injustice. Drawing on Fraser's (2007) idea of citizenship in a "transnational public sphere," we call for a citizenship that transcends boundaries and breaks down hierarchies of publics by resisting narratives of domination and manipulation:

> If citizenship represents a normative guide for leading an engaged, meaningful, and active life, then the ethical concept of sustainability forms a foundational basis for rethinking the rights, requirements, and responsibilities of citizenship in a global context.
>
> (Kurian et al., 2014, p. 437)

The discourses of both sustainability and citizenship are founded on democratic ideals; yet underlying them both are several dialectical tensions. In earlier work, we have identified six axes of such tensions: (1) rights and responsibilities, (2) state and non-state, (3) public and private, (4) human and non-human nature, (5) universal and particular, and (6) democracy and capitalism (Kurian et al., 2014). Describing a dialectical tension as "a system of oppositions that logically or functionally negate one another," Baxter and Scharp (2016, p. 1) point out that "communication is not merely a way to manage contradictions, but the very act of communication is understood as a contradictory process of meaning-making" (p. 2). Public relations has long been conceived in dichotomous terms (e.g., functional or discursive; good or evil; or marked by interests of corporate or activist actors). Yet, viewing public relations as a process for radical social change envisages moving it past dichotomies to resist actively entrenched ideas that align with dominant publics as a default setting. Martin and Nakayama (1999) show how a dialectical perspective "emphasizes the relational, rather than individual aspects and persons" (p. 14). Building on this premise, we argue that public relations as sustainable citizenship goes beyond a conception of public relations serving the interests of particular organizations, be they corporate ones or activist ones, to a process of building relationships among publics that are unrepresented in mainstream discourses. Dialectical thinking, therefore, "is inherently political and engages with the interstices of contradictory dynamics within social systems" (Munshi & Edwards, 2011, p. 359; see also Mitchell, 2002) and "forces us to move beyond our familiar categories" (Martin & Nakayama, 2010, p. 73).

Building on Edwards's (2012) socio-cultural conception of public relations as "the flow of purposive communication produced on behalf of individuals, formally constituted and informally constituted groups through their continuous transactions with other social entities" (p. 21), we explore how this "flow" of communication resists dominant discourses along the way, highlighting dialectical tensions embedded in discursive struggles. Carried through in this flow of communication is the idea of sustainable citizenship that reaches beyond publics characterized by their dominant organizational or societal affiliations.

In essence, then, public relations as sustainable citizenship is about

* Problematizing power as domination and revealing inequality
* Building solidarity and expanding the political public sphere
* Breaking down hierarchies of publics
* Resisting dominant narratives and creating alternative channels of communication
* Exposing and negotiating dialectical tensions

Sustainable citizenship and public relations

From the point of view of critical public relations, the notion of sustainable citizenship encompasses building active relationships among a variety of publics that actively engage with power and leads to representing the unrepresented. At one level, such a notion stands in opposition to the discourse of what Whitman (2008) calls "corporate citizenship" which is geared towards "supplanting broad community-based democratic participation with narrow and specialized forms of participation based on corporate values" (p. 178). At another level, sustainable citizenship broadens the idea of public participation to include those whose voices are muted or silenced by the high decibel levels of the carefully crafted messages of influential lobby groups.

Infusing a notion of sustainable citizenship into public relations scholarship and practice is a significant challenge. The field has historically been ideologically obsessed with the idea of being a part of the "dominant coalition" (Broom & Dozier, 1986; Grunig & Hunt, 1984; Grunig, 1992). It is this obsession that has aligned public relations with elite publics and, in turn, supressed those that stand up to corporate logic (Dutta-Bergman, 2005; Munshi & Kurian, 2005). The dominant coalition is not just a group of people with decision-making powers in organizations; it represents the neo-colonial agenda of Western market-based lobby groups. In mainstream public relations, therefore, "those marginalized sectors of society who don't matter" to neo-colonial agendas "are left out of the discursive space" (Dutta & Pal, 2011, p. 214).

Our idea of sustainable citizenship revolves around a notion of democracy that resists hegemonic power. This form of citizenship encompasses subaltern publics building relationships with each other and crafting radically alternative narratives that challenge structures of power wielded by dominant coalitions. As Dutta and Pal (2011) point out, it is in the "spaces of resistive practices that alternative imaginations of public relations as a field of engagement that imagines the possibilities of structural transformation . . . can become possible" (p. 205). However, creating such spaces entails re-framing what constitutes public relations.

In recent years, there have been significant advances in tracking what Edwards and Hodges (2011) call the "socio-cultural turn" in public relations, marked, for example, by work on public relations imbued by critical perspectives (L'Etang & Pieczka, 2006), postmodern and postcolonial perspectives (McKie & Munshi, 2007), social theory (Edwards, 2016; 2018; Edwards, Ihlen & Sommerville, 2019; Ihlen, van Ruler, & Frederiksson, 2009), and social construction (Mickey, 2003), as well as ideas of democracy (Moloney, 2006) and race (Edwards, 2018; Munshi & Edwards, 2011). Also, as a recent review of public relations literature by Mules (2019) shows, "activism is becoming an increasingly significant field of study," and "activist publics are rapidly becoming more influential in public relations practice," with activist groups "moving from being positioned as undesirable publics who constrain an organisation's ability to accomplish its goals, to being recognised as legitimate publics" (p. 19). Yet, there is still a way to go in looking at public relations as a *process* of resistance.

The idea of conceiving public relations as sustainable citizenship goes a long way in acknowledging actions of resistance in which subaltern publics build relationships with each other and challenge structures of coercive influence wielded by dominant coalitions. Public relations as sustainable citizenship involves a reconfiguration of 'received' reality to open up spaces for subaltern perspectives. It is in such spaces that public relations scholars can find opportunities to "look at the processes and practices involved in participation of marginalized subjects in countercultural movements that exist outside the realm of the very public sphere conceptualized by the civil society projects" (Dutta-Bergman, 2005, p. 286). The three substantive chapters of the book explore sets of social movements around the core resources of air, water, and land to evaluate the potential of public relations as sustainable citizenship, a process that exposes discursive inequalities and dismantles the hierarchies of publics through active resistance and that tackles head-on the dialectical tensions embedded in organizational and societal discourses. Each of these movements engages with power, politics, and solidarity and focuses on the message of resistance as communicative action.

Air, water, and land

We have chosen air, water, and land as three realms of the planet where public relations can (and does) play out as sustainable citizenship, especially if we resist the notion of public relations as the relationship between organizations and their stakeholders and instead see the processes of public relations as being of and for the planet and its inhabitants. Environmental and social justice go hand in hand, and a public relations of and for the planet means recognizing the interests of all of its inhabitants, including the many un- (or under-)represented publics, such as a wide range of Indigenous communities and young people, who either choose to stay out of or are left out of democratic processes. These publics are not necessarily aligned with specific activist groups but are seeking to change the status quo of a world increasingly defined by exploitation, individualization, and overconsumption. The processes of resistance in which they engage do have particular local goals, but they also stand for larger goals of planetary sustainability, addressing, for example, the dialectics of the universal and the particular, the local and the global, and democracy and capitalism. These processes of resistance, often rooted in Indigenous and non-Western traditions, see current issues of climate change, water rights, or land disputes, for example, not as zero-sum games but as broader platforms for action on equity and justice.

Despite the stark scientific and ecological reality, an unholy squad of fossil fuel industries, mass media, conservative think-tanks, primarily in the US, and a handful of contrarian scientists have come together to thwart any kind of meaningful action on climate change. The enormous wealth of the profiteers of global neoliberal capitalism who fund climate denialism or its more recent variant, climatewashing (see Chapter 2), and the resulting political and economic clout they wield (Klein, 2014), has resulted in their extraordinary success in both controlling the message about climate change and paralyzing the possibilities for meaningful action by states. However, it is in the face of such political paralysis on acting against destructive economic policies and practices that we find powerful new voices in the form of the diversely constituted global justice movements. The climate justice movement is growing in leaps and bounds and now comprises thousands of local, regional, national, and global organizations (Foran & Widick, 2013). The movement straddles both the First and Third Worlds. Many of those who champion the cause of addressing climate change argue for a public relations that can build a discourse of urgent action on climate justice. In Chapter 2, we report on the work of a range of such movements around the world, especially in the most vulnerable settings, that seek to shift the narrative.

Alongside the cascading threat of climate change is an intensifying global crisis of freshwater, marked by scarcity, pollution, and depletion of ground water. This crisis is affecting more than two billion people living in water-stressed parts of the planet (Barlow, 2007). Even as access to clean water and sanitation is one more symbol of the great divide between the haves and the have-nots, ground water is rapidly being depleted through indiscriminate "ground water mining" to meet irrigation needs of farming and demands for drinking water. Coordinated struggles against the corporatization of water and inequitable access to this life resource are beginning to cut through the agenda set by dominant elites. The powerful alliances forged by Indigenous and non-Indigenous communities from around the world with the Lakota, Dakota, and Nakota people at Standing Rock Reservation to resist the Dakota Access Pipeline (DAPL) in the US to safeguard their ancient rights to water (see Chapter 3) is an example of how subaltern publics can come together in solidarity to get a radically alternative message of sustainability out to the world. Across the globe, we are also witnessing vocal resistance by environmental activists and members of local communities to the shipping out of millions of litres of pristine water from underground springs by private corporations to boost the profits of the bottled water industry. In Chapter 3, we explore the deployment of alternative and resistive communication strategies by disparate movements as they weave together concerns for cultural identity, social sustainability, and environmental justice in articulating their campaigns over access to water.

Like struggles over the climate and over rights to water, contestations over land are marked to a great degree by unequal battles between the strong-arm tactics of the state and some of its underprivileged citizens. We focus, in Chapter 4, on two land-based conflicts in which marginalized publics are facing up to colonizing narratives. The story of the Middle East (or more accurately West Asia) is dominated by the conflict in Israel-Palestine. The rival claims to the 'holy land' notwithstanding, the state of Israel was created on the platform of a strategically planned and executed public relations campaign by Zionist activists (see, e.g., Toledano & McKie, 2013). The Palestinians have not had the gift of a successful public relations campaign to get their side of the story out. Yet, the links between grassroots activists, Jewish Israeli champions of the Palestinian cause, and human rights groups in different parts of the world are beginning to slowly but steadily make an imprint of their version of history and their narratives of persecution on public minds. The scene of the other set of contemporary struggles over the land, identity, and the meanings of nationhood is India, where the current ruling regime is actively playing the majoritarian card to push the nation's minorities to the wall. The dominant communication device here is that of nationalism, misplaced as it is by the flawed, even fake, conflation of national identity with religious identity. But the resistance against the communication and rationalization of subjugation has been strikingly powerful, bringing together subaltern publics from across the country to reclaim the rights of minorities in a democratic polity.

Discussing communicative struggles against neo-colonial vested interests across the realms of air, water, and land, our book articulates a notion of an insurgent public relations in opposition to conceptions of public relations as merely a manipulative tool of communication management. Such an idea rests on a platform of resistance and solidarity. We focus, of course, on a form of resistance highlighting "participatory processes of communication" that "bring communities together in solidarity" and are "set in opposition to oppressive structural forces" (Dutta, 2012, p. 9). But we also look to a form of resistance that acts "with sufficient intention and purpose to negotiate power relations from below in order to rework them in a more favourable or emancipatory direction" (Chandra, 2015, p. 565). Implicit in the emphasis on negotiation is to invoke in public relations a capacity to abrogate its managerial partisanship and speak truth to power. Active exercises by people invoking self-determination and claiming the rights to their own future (as indeed their own past and present) are essential processes for reconfiguring discourses of power and control. Such processes of reclaiming are also communicative acts. They are not merely about repossessing lands taken over by force or manipulation but also about reclaiming cultural identities and forms of representation (Smith, 2012). In the next chapter, we look at how climate justice movements are coming together to coordinate urgent action on climate change in the face of sophisticated communication strategies of the fossil fuel industries.

2 Air

Breathing life into action
on climate change

The British Museum in London was the venue for two competing kinds of public relations in February 2020. In one, a giant multinational company in active collusion with the museum, itself accused of promoting a narrative of colonization through its repository of art and artefacts plundered from different parts of the world (Peirsson-Hagger, 2019), followed the neo-colonial, capitalist path of promoting its corporate image. In the other, an amorphous group of climate protesters drew attention to a narrative of resistance to corporate interests.

The museum was showcasing what it described as a "phenomenal new exhibition" that tells the story of the ancient city of Troy and its "captivating characters" from "dramatic ancient sculptures and exquisite vase paintings to powerful contemporary works" (British Museum, 2020). It was the name of the exhibition that caught the discerning visitor's eye: "The BP exhibition/ Troy: Myth and reality." There was no need to search for any hidden sub-text or subliminal images. It was out there in bold print: "The BP exhibition." The BP of the pantheon of fossil fuel giants that are facing tumultuous protests from climate change activists around the world. Almost on cue, climate activists, dressed as masked Greek warriors, chose a day for their voice to be heard as they demonstrated on the museum's forecourt along with a wooden horse as a metaphor for the Trojan Horse that laid siege to the city of Troy (Gayle, 2020).

BP's attempts to project itself as a patron of art and culture was part of cleverly constructed corporate promotional strategies that seek to enhance, reduce, re-shape, or manipulate reality to maximize the material value of a product, organization, or even ideology. Of course, BP is not alone in executing this kind of public relations. There is a long history of public relations strategies used by fossil fuel companies fomenting misinformation, undermining climate science, practising greenwashing, and manipulating the media, that have confused the public (Cook, Supran, Lewandowsky,

Oreskes, & Maibach, 2019) and helped paralyze the possibilities for meaningful action by governments driven by narrowly defined ideas of 'national
interest.' They followed the precedent set by the tobacco industry of delib-
erate deception to prevent any attempt at regulating it (Cook et al., 2019;
Oreskes & Conway, 2011; Union of Concerned Scientists, 2007). The petro-
leum industry knew perhaps as early as the 1950s that increasing carbon
emissions from burning fossil fuels would lead to global temperature rise
but chose to hide the fact. From the 1990s until the 2010s, ExxonMobil, BP,
Shell, Chevron, and other industry actors actively fomented climate denialism, funding conservative think-tanks, 'astroturf' (fake) advocacy groups,
and a select group of scientists to spread lies about climate science (Bond,
2012; Cook et al., 2019).

In more recent years, the public relations strategies of the fossil fuel industry have become more and more sophisticated, moving from the already
well-critiqued phases of 'greenwashing' to what we call 'youthwashing'
and 'democracywashing' – indeed, a wholesale 'climatewashing.' In the
context of the global crisis of climate change, such strategies, initiated and
executed by colluding corporate and political elites, seek to colonize and
subvert the culture – the norms, values, desires, and behaviours – of groups
of people in society through actions that mimic green ideals, youth aspirations, or democratic principles.

The catastrophic phenomenon of climate change is one of the markers
of the age of the Anthropocene, an epoch marked by human domination
of the earth (Crutzen & Stoermer, 2000; Subramaniam, 2019), creating
the prospect for a systems failure of the planet (Kurian, 2017). Yet, rather
than seeing this crisis and the linked crises of species extinction, freshwater
degradation and depletion, and soil erosion, among others, as an inevitable consequence of *being human*, a historically grounded analysis would
reveal these multiple crises as driven by the interlocking forces of colonization, capitalism, and empire (see, e.g., Ghosh, 2016; Haraway et al., 2016),
while applying a gender lens would bring into focus the "material or discursive effects" of the "intersection of hegemonic masculinities and climate
change" (MacGregor, 2019, p. 61).

Recognizing the historical specificity and the gendered nature of the
creation of these crises allows us to ask not only what drive and sustain
them today but also how they can be resisted and overcome. What are the
networks of power, politics, policies, and practices that helped create and
sustain the climate emergency we face today? What communicative strategies have helped those hegemonic forces to shape "that period when the
accumulation of carbon in the atmosphere was rewriting the destiny of the
earth" (Ghosh, 2016, p. 7)? And what counter-forces – of grassroots civic
activism by youth, the Indigenous, poor women, and by environmental and

social movements and non-governmental organizations (NGOs) – are being mobilized to enact a form of public relations and sustainable citizenship for planetary sustainability?

In this chapter, we outline how the toxic fumes of unethical public relations by powerful actors and beneficiaries of the current extractivist high-carbon economy have vitiated the planet's air, both literally and metaphorically, and unpack some key elements of North-South tensions and the technocratic managerialism that mark the policy tools of the United Nations Framework Convention on Climate Change (UNFCCC), the overarching international environmental treaty guiding the global response to the climate crisis. We then go on to show how climate movements, marshalled especially by Indigenous peoples and youth, are building solidarity with a variety of publics to expand the democratic spaces of deliberative politics globally and locally, and challenging the hegemony of corporate and political elites.

Domains of subterfuge: greenwashing, youthwashing, and democracywashing

The start of the second decade of the 21st century is marked by clashing forces around a warming world – the continued delaying and obfuscating strategies of the fossil fuel industries and their political and economic allies, on the one hand (Holden, 2020), and the rise of people's movements everywhere demanding a change to status quo-oriented politics and policies on the other (Bhavnani, Foran, Kurian, & Munshi, 2019). The grim portents of a climate changed world are everywhere, seen in the unprecedented fires in Australia in 2019–2020 that have killed over 30 people and an estimated billion animals (Flanagan, 2020; Cox, 2020), and the floods, droughts, and storms across Africa and Asia that have wreaked havoc on lives, livelihoods, housing, and food crops and driven the concomitant migration of people. Yet, even such stark realities appear to do little to give impetus to either national or global-level governmental actions. We see, for example, politicians in Australia still in thrall to fossil fuel interests, holding on to climate denialism even as their country burns (Flanagan, 2020). At the same time, global climate policy-making processes continue in a state of near paralysis, as evident at the 25th Conference of the Parties (COP 25) in Madrid in December 2019, with little progress on commitments to cut emissions to meet the goal of 1.5 or even 2 degrees C temperature rise, carbon market mechanisms, or accountability for historical emissions (Chandrasekhar, 2019; Narain, 2019).

How do we explain such lack of action on climate change? As a series of investigations, reports, and academic analyses have made clear, wealthy fossil fuel companies have created "an infrastructure of persuasion" (Monbiot, 2020) that has succeeded in thwarting meaningful action on climate change (Hoggan & Littlemore, 2010). The political and economic clout of those who fund climate denialism (Klein, 2014) has resulted in their extraordinary success in controlling the message about climate change.

Scientific consensus on anthropogenic climate change became established through the 1990s, and, in fact, a series of studies in the 2000s demonstrated that up to 97% of published papers on climate change take anthropogenic climate change as a given (Oreskes, 2004; Cook et al., 2013). But, as is now well established, corporate interests chose to attack this consensus by attempting to undermine the state of climate science not only by emphasizing "uncertainties" and engaging in greenwashing but also by manipulating the media "to give attention to 'both sides'" (Cook et al., 2019, p. 7). The news media's commitment to "balance" also meant that even credible news organizations such as the BBC provided a platform to denialists (Boykoff & Boykoff, 2004; Cook et al., 2019; Oreskes & Conway, 2011). The denialist techniques span the use of "fake experts, logical fallacies, impossible expectations, cherry picking, and conspiracy theories" (Cook et al., 2019, p. 10). The network of climate denialism includes

> fossil fuel companies, utilities, ancillary manufacturers, trade associations, PR firms, advertising agencies, libertarian foundations, think-tanks, legal firms and individuals, all feeding an echo chamber of pundits, astroturf groups, blogs, media and, yes, politicians.
>
> (Supran & Oreskes, 2020)

Now that public opinion is beginning to see through denialism and there is an upsurge of global concern about climate change, fossil fuel companies are changing to more subtle forms of appropriating the discourse, which we call 'climatewashing.' The process of greenwashing (e.g., Delmas & Burbano, 2011; Marquis, Toffel, & Zhou, 2016) is, of course, well known as a form of appropriating the sustainability discourse. BP in fact has invested in an expensive advertising campaign claiming that it is embracing renewables to address the climate crisis. Described by *Campaign* magazine as the "biggest corporate campaign since before the Deepwater Horizon oil spill of 2010" (Gwynn, 2019), this promotional push across print, television, and digital platforms focuses on how the company is moving ahead in environmentally responsible ways. BP's director of brand, Duncan Blake, is quoted in *Campaign* as saying that the push was "in response to the changing energy landscape – the mix has been changing quite rapidly and that's been driven by changes in tech and environmental concerns" (Gwynn, 2019). Yet, environmental lawyers, who have complained against the campaign, have called it a "smokescreen" (Laville, 2019). Sophie Marjanac, a lawyer for ClientEarth, told *The Guardian* that

> while BP's advertising focuses on clean energy, in reality, more than 96% of the company's annual capital expenditure is on oil and gas. According to its own figures, BP is spending less than £4 in every £100 on low-carbon investments each year. The rest is fuelling the climate crisis.
>
> (Laville, 2019)

Similarly, Shell launched a huge campaign in 2019 to "invest in natural ecosystems" to act on global climate change (Shell, 2019). But, as Monbiot (2019) cautions, "Shell is not a green saviour." The company's "'cash engines,' according to its annual report, are oil and gas," he says. Emphasizing that "there is no sign that it plans to turn the engines off," Monbiot (2019) goes on to say that the company's "growth priorities are chemical production and deep water oil extraction," and while "it does list low-carbon energy among its 'emerging opportunities' in future decades," it is committed to developing them "alongside fracking and liquefied fossil gas technologies." Continuing on this greenwashing trajectory, the Norwegian multinational Statoil strategically dropped the word 'oil' from its name, changing it to Equinor in 2018 (Walsgard & Holter, 2018). The renamed company, however, continues "drilling the Arctic" (Bell, 2020).

With global youth movements demanding climate action gaining ground all over the world (discussed later in the chapter), fossil fuel companies have launched a public relations offensive to win over young people. Even as the charismatic Swedish schoolgirl Greta Thunberg castigated global political leaders at the United Nations Climate Action Summit for "stealing my dreams and my childhood with your empty words" (Vaughan, 2019), CEOs of fossil fuel companies were making attempts to seduce young people into their fold. As Brown (2019) reports, CEOs from BP, Royal Dutch Shell, and Equinor, among others, were at the Oil and Gas Climate Initiative's conference in New York where a lunch event was organized to "'explore options for long-term engagement' with young people the industry could trust." The event, facilitated by "Student Energy, a nonprofit based in Alberta, near Canada's tar sands region," set aside "time for students to grill the CEOs about their inaction on climate change" (Brown, 2019). The fossil fuel industry evidently sees events like this as textbook public relations for the sector. Instead of denying climate change as they used to do, industry leaders are communicating with young people, sponsoring them for green events, and offering them opportunities, funding, and even prospects for eventual employment while simultaneously pursuing proposals to continue extracting carbon-intensive fuels and products. Brown (2019), cit-ing many youth activists, describes this new trend of reaching out to young people as "youthwashing." Young people are acutely aware of the market-ing trend of appropriating youth launched by the giants of greenhouse gas emissions, and, as Eilidh Robb (2019) of the UK Youth Climate Coalition says, the coalition has started a public campaign of its own, "calling out the misuse of youth on our new twitter account (@youthwashing)."

In addition, corporate promotional machines are also indulging in what we call 'democracywashing' with corporations forming coalitions with political elites, designing elaborate campaigns for stakeholder engagement and participating in events that are ostensibly geared to listening to public voices. Such strategies reflect the practice of what Cronin (2018) has called "commercial democracy":

> While corporations are diluting or distorting democracy by exerting strong influence over government through lobbying, shaping regula-tory standards, and becoming government consultants. . . [they are] simultaneously taking over the terrain of the social contract by offering the public representation, voice, and agency.
>
> (p. 44)

Take, for example, Chevron's boast of being part of the rescue mission in the recent fires in Australia through its $1m donation to the Australian Red Cross (it is another matter that this amount is just 0.00667% of its annual earnings) or Exxon Australia's exhortation to people to "Stay safe and have fun" (Supran & Oreskes, 2020). Campaigns run by fossil fuel companies to show their commitment to renewable energy and protecting the planet, ranging from ExxonMobil's commercials about its investments in algae fuels and Chevron's promotion of electric car charging, claim to listen to the concerns of people and create a better future for them. But the truth is, of course, a lot murkier. All of these companies are not only continu-ing their (fossil fuel) business as usual but extending their influence over business and political networks. Shareholder democracy has already been undermined by the US Securities and Exchange Commission's announce-ment of a "new rule that would make it much harder for shareholders to file proposals on climate change and other environmental, social, and govern-ance issues with publicly traded US companies" (Mulvey, Allen, & Frum-hoff, 2019). These companies have also co-opted political leaders in selling neatly packaged announcements to the media and the public about invest-ments in renewable energy and the planet.

The billions that the industry has spent in funding politicians has allowed it to control political institutions while simultaneously subverting the language of environmentalism. Thus, stories about commitments to renewable energy and the planet are offered to the media and the general public while hiding the continued push for fossil fuel investments. For example, British Prime Minister Boris Johnson, at the opening of the UK-Africa investment summit in London on 20 January 2020, stated:

> We all breathe the same air, we live beneath the same sky, and we all suffer when carbon emissions rise and the planet warms. So from today, the British government will no longer provide any new direct official development assistance, investment, export credit or trade promotion for thermal coal mining or coal power plants overseas. To put it simply, not another penny of UK taxpayers' money will be directly invested in digging up coal or burning it for electricity. Instead, we're going to focus on supporting the transition to lower- and zero-carbon alternatives.
>
> (Johnson, 2020)

Yet, as *The Guardian* reported, "More than 90% of the £2bn in energy deals struck at this week's UK-Africa investment summit were for fossil fuels" (Carrington, 2020). British investments in countries across Africa announced at the summit span oil, gas, gold mining, and airlines, all of which illustrate the powerful grip of a high-carbon status quo. Commenting on the bid for African markets in the name of development at the summit, Nick Dearden, director of the advocacy group Global Justice Now, noted how similar it was to the "scramble for Africa" disguised as a humanitarian project in the 19th century (cited in Carrington, 2020).

Indeed, Johnson's actions reflect what Ghosh (2016) has argued – that climate change is a reflection of empire: "The British Empire was essentially built on fossil fuels: It was the British mastery of coal that gave it a huge military advantage over the rest of the world" (Ghosh cited in Knight, 2019). In so many ways, the neoliberal communication landscape of contemporary times is similar to that of the colonial era. Anne McClintock's (1995) description of colonial advertising is telling: "colonial heroes and colonial scenes were emblazoned on a host of domestic commodities, from milk cartons to sauce bottles, . . . toffee boxes to baking powder" (p. 219). She shows how

> in the flickering magic lantern of imperial desire, teas, biscuits, tobaccos, Bovril, tins of cocoa and, above all, soaps beach themselves on far-flung shores, tramp through jungles, quell uprisings, restore order and write the inevitable legend of commercial progress across the colonial landscape.
>
> (p. 219)

As McKie and Munshi (2007) say,

> What is common to the colonial and neo-colonial communication strategies of powerful institutions, whether empires or corporate giants, is the core emphasis on promoting Western business and/or political interests but concealing their selfish goals under a gloss of universal good and benevolence.

(p. 64)

The nexus of capitalism, colonialism, and empire – driven by a Western masculinist ideology, as ecofeminist scholars have long argued (Sturgeon, 1997; Gaard, 2015) – thus continues to wedge the high-carbon economy in deeper as self-serving commitments to short-term growth and the desire to hold on to geopolitical power override any notion of a 'green new deal,' let alone a radical transformation of economy, society, and politics. This was evident at the World Economic Forum at Davos in January 2020 where US Treasury Secretary Steven Mnuchin dismissed calls for fossil fuel divestment and elimination of carbon emissions from youth climate activists by invoking the slogan of "development" for the Third World (Wearden, 2020a).

The desire to provide electricity to the developing world is a mere rhetorical device to delay addressing climate change in the interest of dominant business and political elites. The lack of urgency in taking necessary climate action, as well as the inadequacy of the actions that are committed to, can also be seen in the UNFCCC processes, especially in the work of the Conference of the Parties (COP), to review the implementation of global treaties on climate action in annual meetings. Although the principle of 'common but differentiated responsibilities' (CBDR), central to the UNFCCC and also seen in the Kyoto Protocol of 1997 and the Paris Agreement of 2015, reflects a commitment to the idea of equity through the recognition that the wealthy Global North should make significant and immediate reductions to greenhouse gas (GHG) emissions given their historical responsibility for creating the climate crisis, the wealthy states have failed to abide by it. The US, most notably, has refused to acknowledge responsibility for historical emissions and has spurned the 'polluter pays' principle. This refusal exemplifies a form of "environmental colonialism" (Agarwal & Narain, 1991). In promoting the narrow national and economic interests of the publics of wealthy states to continue to disproportionately consume global resources and the carbon cake, the US and other wealthy states such as Australia, Canada, and oil-producing Saudi Arabia have sought to marginalize the struggles for survival of subaltern Third World publics.

At the same time, governments of rapidly developing Third World states, such as the BASIC countries of Brazil, South Africa, India, and China, have demanded "equitable space for development" (PTI, 2010) as well as finance, technology, and capacity-building support from the Global North – even as they increasingly faced criticism from the most vulnerable states, such as the Pacific Islands and other small island states for their unwillingness to take pro-active steps to transition away from fossil fuel-driven economic development (*Down to Earth*, 2011).

In the context of the international global system, it is important to recognize the layers of hegemony at play. Resource-rich First World states dominate and drive the UN COP process, ensuring by their strategic manipulations, actions, and refusals the protection of their national interest through limiting any real efforts to cut emissions – and profiteering from those limited efforts. The Global South, a vast and diversely situated set of states, has its own competing agendas, with the BASIC countries, for example, continuing carbon-intensive development despite the impacts of climate change on the most vulnerable peoples both in their own countries and elsewhere. In essence, dominant and subaltern publics exist both in international and intra-national contexts, demonstrating how power is problematized in different ways at different levels through challenging existing hierarchies of publics and opening up the public and political spheres.

Climate justice movements as acts of resistance

The power imbalance between wealthy nations and poorer nations, and the consequent climate implications for people living in such a divided world, as well as the disproportionate influence of multinational fossil fuel companies and allied businesses in shaping dominant narratives that marginalize subaltern publics in global contexts, has led to demands for climate justice:

> Climate justice perspectives center the fact that the brunt of climate change falls hardest on the most poor and marginal peoples – peoples often trampled upon by the twin ravages of colonialism and capitalism, who demonstrate resilience despite these depredations.
>
> (Munshi, Kurian, Foran, & Bhavnani, 2019, p. 3)

The idea of climate justice emerged as a fundamental concept to challenge North-South inequities in the UN COP process. Emerging around the time of COP 13 in 2007 in Bali, Indonesia, it started to build momentum amongst activists and NGOs from the Global North and South, as well as among negotiators from the developing world (Roberts & Parks, 2009; Ott, Sterk, & Watanabe, 2008).

As the idea of climate justice grew, pulling in grassroots movements involving activists working on development, the environment, and social issues, as well as NGOs, civil society actors, and politicians, new strategies and discourses emerged. For example, to challenge the dominant perspective that the Third World was equally culpable for climate change through their GHG emissions, the idea of "ecological debt" incurred by the First World through their GHG emissions was put forward by environmental activists, academics, and Third World states (see, e.g., Bond, 2012; Martinez-Alier, 2003; Narain, 2009; Roberts & Parks, 2009) with a demand that wealthy nations repay their debt to the Global South. Using climate debt as a negotiating framework for a climate treaty was a key demand of several states in the lead-up to the Copenhagen COP in 2009, representing a significant attempt to shift the nature of climate treaty negotiation discourse, albeit with limited success (Bond, 2012). This message that "industrialized nations along with private sector polluters have an obligation to remedy ecological debt" has continued to be articulated and amplified by climate justice organizations (Finley-Brook, 2014, p. 11), helping transform the nature of public discourse on climate policy.

Distinct from the efforts of Third World states to seek equity in global climate diplomacy and policy-making are grassroots climate justice movements, which include in their fold numerous peasant and Indigenous movements across the Global North and South. Many of these climate action movements reflect a public relations based on solidarity of Indigenous peoples, poor women, peasants, fisherfolk, and forest peoples around the world who have already witnessed climate change extremes and have begun the painful process of forced adaptation. We examine specific instances of how Indigenous movements and youth climate movements have problematized power, expanded the political public sphere, and disrupted dominant narratives with radical, insurgent narratives of their own, thereby embodying and enacting sustainable citizenship.

Seeing REDD

A prime example of the UNFCCC's neoliberal, capitalist use of market mechanisms such as emissions trading is Reducing Emissions from Deforestation and forest Degradation (REDD), which was launched at COP 13 in 2007 and expanded by 2008 as REDD+ to include not only forest degradation but also "conservation, sustainable management of forests, and enhancement of forest carbon stocks in developing countries" (UNFCCC, n.d.) as ways to mitigate GHG emissions. In essence, REDD+ is a policy mechanism for protecting forests by providing financial incentives to owners to preserve them and allowing wealthy corporations and states who pay for that forest preservation to offset their own carbon emissions. Article 5 of the Paris Agreement encourages all countries to implement and support REDD+, and there are an estimated 344 active projects across 56 countries (Milne et al., 2019), demonstrating the widespread support for this initiative among states, corporations, some NGOs and scientists, among others. For instance, a senior scientist with the World Resources Institute stated:

> REDD+ has also catalyzed national dialogues that have highlighted the inequitable outcomes of business-as-usual forest management. In several countries, including Indonesia, such dialogues have strengthened the position of indigenous peoples and given them a voice in national policy arenas they didn't previously have. . . . REDD+ will also help countries put into place policies, markets, recognition of indigenous rights, and other governance structures that allow them to manage forests for all their many benefits.
>
> (Seymour, n.d.)

In contrast to this positive reading, others including Indigenous peoples, activists, and social scientists have offered a very different take on REDD+ (see, e.g., Atmadja & Verchot, 2011; deShazo, Pandey, & Smith, 2016; Girvan, 2017; Milne et al., 2019). For example, they point to the flaws inherent in the central logic of using "market mechanisms or economic incentives to compel state, non-state and local actors to conserve carbon stocks by avoiding deforestation and forest degradation" in developing countries (Milne et al., 2019, p. 85), which demonstrates the dominance of technocratic, Western science-dominated approaches to climate management that serve to further marginalize Indigenous and peasant peoples through new forms of control over their lands and resources (Girvan, 2017). As Girvan (2017) comments:

> While it is important to recognize the importance of trees and soil and their relations with carbon in efforts to avoid deforestation, the (partial) recovery of forests as 'carbon sinks' may initiate new forms of colonial dispossession.
>
> (p. 1044)

Indeed, a recent academic analysis of REDD+ projects points out that such projects have contributed to social conflict and done little to prevent forest loss and degradation (Milne et al., 2019). This reading corroborates the larger critique of carbon markets as a whole that are, as Böhm (2013) explains, beset by corruption and lack of transparency and are fuelling practices that undermine sustainable local economies – while not reducing carbon emissions in any way. In addition, a cross-national study across

Mozambique, Nepal, Tanzania, and Vietnam of gender implications of REDD+ demonstrated that despite women's important role in forest management, they were "frequently marginalised from decision-making in communities" (Macqueen, 2013), a conclusion reinforced by a finding that living on a REDD site was associated with a decline in women's wellbeing (Larson et al., 2018).

There is now a sustained campaign against REDD+, led by Indigenous people's movements such as the Global Alliance Against REDD and the No-REDD website, to systematically challenge the dominant neo-colonial and managerial narratives that promote such mitigation measures. In a powerful refutation of the dominant discourse, Ninawa Huni Kui, president of the Huni Kui people of Acre in Brazil, stated in an interview with *Democracy Now*:

> REDD is not a solution to climate change. It is a false solution to climate change. And furthermore, indigenous peoples are not the ones that are causing climate change. In Brazil, in Mato Grosso, the biggest soy baron is receiving funding and subsidies from the Brazilian government to cut down forests. This is not a solution to climate change. And furthermore, REDD is criminalizing us. And really, if they care about real solutions, they've got to talk to the logging companies, the soy barons, the corporations that are polluting and destroying nature. Indigenous peoples protect Mother Earth. We defend our mother, because she is our mother, because she gives us food. She gives us the air that we breathe. She gives us the Amazon. And the Amazon is important not just for indigenous peoples; it's important for the whole world.
>
> (Ninawa Huni Kui, 2014)

Similarly, the campaign raised its voice at the United Nations Permanent Forum on Indigenous Issues in May 2016 to denounce the Paris Agreement as merely a pathway to privatization of land and resources:

> The Paris Agreement is a trade agreement, nothing more. It promises to privatize, commodify and sell forest and agriculture lands as carbon offsets in fraudulent schemes such as REDD+. These offset scams provide financial laundering mechanisms for developed countries to launder their carbon pollution in the Global South.
>
> (Global Alliance Against REDD+, 2016)

Thus, the campaign has been able to keep a clear focus on the injustice being perpetuated on Indigenous people through climate change policies and schemes that force them to shoulder the disproportionate burden of addressing climate change, including the loss of control over their land and resources. The Indigenous Environmental Network's (IEN) (n.d.) website on REDD+ provides a record of stories around the violence that Indigenous and other marginalized groups around the world have experienced in the context of REDD+ projects, and the mobilization and alliances being built among, for example, "forest people, rubber tappers" in Brazil. IEN, most notably, has articulated a central message that is now starting to permeate and influence more mainstream environmental discourses: that there can be no carbon offsets if irreversible climate change is to be avoided, and, in fact, unless we move towards no carbon emissions and build decentralized, sustainable, and equitable societies and economies, there will be no habitable earth for any of us – humans and non-humans.

The work of building a global alliance that has maintained and sustained the opposition to REDD+ epitomizes the key tenets of public relations as sustainable citizenship, including, for example, problematizing power and revealing inequality, resisting dominant narratives and channels of communication, expressing solidarity, and exposing and negotiating dialectical tensions between market mechanisms of reducing emissions and building sustainable frameworks for justice-oriented action on climate change.

This movement's successful resistance of the dominant discourses of consumption is an example of the transformation of Indigenous peoples from being seen as "victims of the effects of climate change" to "agents of environmental conservation" (Etchart, 2017). Despite being agents of change, Indigenous communities do not act in the interests of specific organizations but are nodal points in a web of resistance that builds relationships among subaltern publics marginalized by the systemic assumptions of hierarchies of publics in democratic systems influenced by capitalism. Indigenous peoples themselves are diverse, and the very use of the plural 'peoples' is "a way of recognizing that there are real differences between different indigenous peoples" but they "belong to a network of peoples" and

> share experiences as peoples who have been subjected to the colonization of their lands and cultures, and the denial of their sovereignty, by a colonizing society that has come to dominate and determine the shape and quality of their lives, even after it has formally pulled out.
>
> (Smith, 2012, p. 7)

Indeed, Indigenous climate justice movements "are distinct in their putting resistance to the nexus of colonialism, capitalism, and industrialization at the vanguard of their work" (Whyte, 2019, p. 20), negotiating the dialectics of democracy and capitalism and creating models of citizenship committed to protecting the planet and all its people.

For more than the Greta good

Alongside the work of IEN and other Indigenous activists are the actions taken by youth, including most recently school children from around the world who have reached out to diverse publics and mobilized millions of people around the world to demand a system change to address the climate crisis. Cutting through the noise of corporate climate greenwashing, weak state response, and the inadequacy of global climate policies offered up by the UN COP process, the School Strike for Climate offers a powerful challenge to business as usual. Inspired by Greta Thunberg, who decided in August 2018 to skip school on Fridays to protest outside the Swedish parliament, the School Strike for Climate has sought action by governments to prevent or reverse climate change, keep fossil fuels in the ground, transition to renewable energy, and commit to climate justice (Climate Strike, n.d.). The movement has captured the world's imagination with impromptu climate marches in 6,500 cities around the world on 27 September 2019 alone, drawing in people who had never participated in any form of activism before. We heard the persuasive appeal of the simple but powerful words of Thunberg on a wet February morning in Bristol, UK, where tens of thousands of the young and the old crammed every inch of space in the city's College Green. She took politicians and elected officials to task for their empty rhetoric:

> And still this emergency is being completely ignored by politicians, the media and those in power. Basically nothing is being done to halt this crisis, despite all the beautiful words and promises from the elected officials.
>
> (Thunberg, 2020)

Calling for action on climate change, the determined teenager said that she would not stand aside and watch: "I will not be silenced while the world is on fire – will you?"

Thunberg, however, was only one of many catalysts of the movement for collective action on climate change. The movement is neither restricted to narrow interests of a specific organization nor is it directed by specific actors. It is the organic process of mobilization that makes it public relations as sustainable citizenship. It is not the actor but the action of building solidarity that defines the movement. Thunberg is neither the only young person nor even the first to have reached out to publics with the message of collective action. Youth involvement in global environmental issues has a history that goes back nearly three decades. In 1992, 12-year-old Severn Cullis-Suzuki, a Canadian environmental activist, addressed the UN

Conference on Environment and Development at Rio de Janeiro, calling the delegates to account for the lack of action on environmental degradation, species extinction, child poverty, and wasteful consumerism (Cullis-Suzuki, 1992). A number of treaties did emerge from the Rio Conference, including Agenda 21 and the UNFCCC, among others, but that moment of hope dissipated quickly. Youth involvement in the UN COPs began in earnest in 1999 at COP 5 in Bonn, and in subsequent years, there have been parallel youth and children's conferences that have issued statements and declarations calling on states to act on climate change. For example, at COP 7 in Marrakech, youth organizations called for a move to a "low carbon-emitting future" and the implementation of the Kyoto Protocol (IISD, 2001). Recognized as a constituency by the UNFCCC secretariat before COP 15 in 2009 at Copenhagen, 'YOUNGO' opened up participation to youth delegates from around the world.

Yet, the early youth interventions at COPs did not quite steer states to take concrete actions on climate change. As mentioned earlier in this chapter, the UN has been accused of actively participating in 'youthwashing' not only by sidelining the contributions of youth perspectives but also by opening up the COP space to fossil fuel companies, who actively seek to influence and shape the treaties and agreements being negotiated. Indeed, the failure of COP 15 to make any kind of meaningful progress paved the way for more confrontational politics by youth activists as a palpable sense of frustration and anger developed. At COP 17 in 2011 in Durban, Canadian youth activist Anjali Appadurai, the last speaker at the final open session of the conference, denounced the inaction by states:

> I speak for more than half the world's population. We are the silent majority. You've given us a seat in this hall, but our interests are not on the table. What does it take to get a stake in this game? Lobbyists? Corporate influence? Money? You've been negotiating all my life. In that time, you've failed to meet pledges, you've missed targets, and you've broken promises. But you've heard this all before.
>
> (*Democracy Now*, 2011)

Appadurai's participation in an 'unsanctioned protest' at Durban saw her banned by the UN from future COPs – a decision that was reversed only after significant pressure was brought on the organization and only after Appadurai was forced to sign "a declaration promising to behave" (Leahy, 2013). Thus, even as senior officials of the UN were stating publicly that they welcomed youth participants to participate and speak up, they, along with national government representatives, were simultaneously cracking down on any form of dissent or protest that challenged the status quo

(Appadurai in Leahy, 2013; *Democracy Now*, 2011). The pressures brought on activists – youth and others from trade unions, social movements, and environmental NGOs – to conform to rigid norms of behaviour at the COPs were met with resistance as they sought to retain their presence inside the COPs even as they raised their voices against the political paralysis on display before them. In 2013, at COP 19 in Warsaw, 800 participants from civil society organizations walked out of the COP in a first ever mass withdrawal to protest the lack of ambition, the reneging by developed states on commitments to cut emissions, and the capture of the COP by fossil fuel interests (Vidal & Harvey, 2013).

It is against this background of years of seemingly futile participation by youth and other civil society organizations in the UN COPs that we see the dramatic escalation of vocal climate protests globally in 2018 by youth. They have been supported by numerous other climate activist groups, including Extinction Rebellion (XR), a global movement involved with street protests to press governments to declare a climate emergency. In doing so, these young people have dramatically expanded the political public sphere by claiming the space from which children and youth, as non-voting citizens, have traditionally been excluded and broken down the hierarchies of publics by directly calling out decades of greenwashing and inaction by states and fossil fuel corporations. They have exposed politicians who "have known the truth about climate change" and have "willingly handed over our future to profiteers whose search for quick cash threatens our very existence" (Thunberg, 2019). They have also succeeded in showing up right-wing media commentators, used to dismissing the young as ignorant, by their mastery of climate science and of the recommendations of climate scientists found in the Intergovernmental Panel on Climate Change (IPCC) reports. As a German youth activist Luisa Neubauer pointed out, their demands to shut down carbon emissions, stop extractivist industries, and transition to a post-carbon economy was "not a radical demand [but] a rational demand" (cited in Wearden, 2020b). Young people have channelled the anger of their generation, speaking of betrayal by the adults responsible for the planetary chaos unfolding already:

> You have stolen my dreams and my childhood with your empty words. And yet I'm one of the lucky ones. People are suffering. People are dying. Entire ecosystems are collapsing. We are in the beginning of a mass extinction. And all you can talk about is money and fairytales of eternal economic growth. How dare you!
>
> (Thunberg, address to the UN Climate Summit, September 2019)

This powerful message has resonated globally, but it is also important to note that while Thunberg is an iconic young activist in the West, there are young people in other parts of the world who have been inspiring action as well. Some of these non-Western activists have been centring justice, equity, and equality in the climate action movement and focusing on everyday people and their actions. In the spirit of democratic ideals, climate activists are not homogenous and indeed have diverse perspectives on the central message for action. For example, Sampathkumar (2019) describes how Jamie Margolin, a 17-year-old Colombian American activist, told her that Thunberg's focus "to follow the recommendations of the Intergovernmental Panel on Climate Change's report or deprive future generations – is still the message of an activist from a relatively privileged country," whereas for many others, the reality of climate change means that their "community is literally dying." Similarly, India's Licypriya Kangujam, who at eight years of age was the youngest climate activist to attend COP 25 in Madrid in 2019, has pointed out that she was already an activist at the age of six before Thunberg had started her protest, and has been urging the Indian prime minister to pass a national climate law. Kangujam, too, has called out the media's obsession with Thunberg, commenting: "If you call me 'Greta of India,' you are not covering my story. You are deleting a story" (cited in Taskin, 2020).

As a model of public relations in the spirit of sustainable citizenship, the climate movement has demonstrated the power of diverse publics mobilizing action in their own diverse ways and yet building spontaneous momentum to get the powers that be to address climate change. Many young people have aligned themselves to a number of groups such as 350.org, Global Power Shift, Friends of the Earth, Gen Zero, Climate Action Network, and XR to disrupt the status quo in local context-specific ways while also participating in social justice movements, including Black Lives Matter and #MeToo. Many other young people have remained unaligned with formal groups but have been part of sustained action by subaltern publics such as Indigenous communities. Young people, for example, have been a significant part of Inuit and Cree communities in Labrador resisting the Muskrat Falls hydroelectric project in Canada as well as "Indigenous-led environmental action against colonial energy projects around the world, including work in Karen communities in Thailand, Indigenous peoples in Colombia, Waorani peoples in Ecuador, among Saami peoples and countless other Indigenous nations" (Curnow & Helferty, 2019). A remarkable feature of the youth climate justice protests and actions is the leadership of women as well as the diversity of the participants – transforming the male domination of mainstream environmental activism of the past (Kaplan, 2019). In many ways, young people's willingness to act collectively and work in solidarity to push for environmental and social change embodies feminist and Arend-tian conceptions of power and empowerment.

Radically different from mainstream public relations that depends on carefully calibrated strategies, the unprecedented mass mobilization of young people has shown how organic, often spontaneous movements can foster the building of relationships among diverse publics on a platform of resistance. As O'Brien, Selboe, and Hayward (2018) say, youth are inter-rogating power relationships in "three interrelated ways of dissenting from the policies, systems, and relationships that contribute to climate change: dutiful dissent, disruptive dissent, and dangerous dissent" (p. 4). Accord-ing to these scholars, dutiful dissent is expressed through already-existing forums such as political parties or NGOs; disruptive dissent manifests itself in the attempts to restructure existing systems, overhaul laws and regula-tions, and devise campaigns that explicitly draw attention to issues of equity and justice; and dangerous dissent involves radical movements to gener-ate "new and alternative systems, new ways of doing things, new types of economic relationships, and new ways of organizing society" (O'Brien et al. 2018, p. 6). They clarify that the classifications in the typology are "not based on the motivations or intentions of youth, but rather on the ways youth dissent(ers) could be seen from the perspective of those with political power" (O'Brien et al., 2018, p. 2). The use of the word "danger" therefore symbolizes the threat political and business elites see in youth movements. From the point of view of the young people, their actions are ones of resist-ance where they generate their own agency in the face of powerful lobby groups and political power, an act of sustainable citizenship. Such forms of resistance are slightly different from agenda-specific activist groups such as XR, which has been leading disruptive civil disobedience activities that have forced the news media to focus attention on their message in a manner the media had never done before (Todd, 2019).

The resistance to dominant forms of public relations by activist groups, of course, should not be romanticized. The rhetoric of a climate emergency promoted by XR does get media attention, but, as Cretney and Nissen (2019) say, such rhetoric can sometimes "provide a fertile ground for regressive politics and securitisation that shut down and foreclose opportunities for democracy, citizen engagement and participation," leading to "disastrous consequences, especially for those already suffering from the injustice and inequalities of capitalism and colonialism" (p. 17; see also Tierney, 2008). As we have seen with the COVID-19 crisis in 2020, many governments have done well to enforce lockdowns to prevent the spread of the virus but at the same time have left vulnerable sections of communities without the necessary resources to survive long spells of economic deprivation. Yet, as Cretney and Nissen (2019) say, crisis narratives do "also have the potential to cleave open space for new engagements with politics and the social landscape, particularly at the community scale" (p. 17), especially in shifting the debate from individual responsibility to collective action.

Public relations as sustainable citizenship engages with the dialectics of the individual and the collective as also the dialectics of democracy and capitalism. As Holmstrom (2018) suggests, the ecological crisis forces us to rethink the notions of individualism and collectivism, with rationality not restricted to the individual domain but seen from a collective perspective as well. Such an approach does not call for the surrender of individual rights but instead seeks democratic ways of planning that go beyond capitalism's obsession with individual ownership. The actions of Indigenous peoples and youth activists – ranging from the spontaneous to the coordinated – have forced open public spaces for alternative visions and stories of climate justice and helped facilitate powerful forms of solidarity. The public relations of the global climate justice movement demonstrates the processes of relationship building among a variety of publics by interrogating and resisting the dynamics of power to clear the air of the fog of a deceptive promotional endeavour that imperils the planet. In the following chapter, we look at the communicative struggles over the life resource of water, including acts of resistance to the neo-colonial discourses of commodifying water.

3   Water
Struggles over defining a life resource

Even as we are writing this chapter in the first half of 2020, the world around us has been struggling to contain the invisible but lethal legions of the COVID-19 virus. The rampant virus has struck the most vulnerable dead, stretching health systems beyond the breaking point, forcing people in every continent into lockdowns, and shattering economies. Public health messages communicated around the world emphasize that one of the most effective ways of protecting against this deadly virus is the simple mix of soap and water (World Health Organization [WHO], 2020), which can neutralize the bundle of ribonucleic acid covered in an envelope of lipid that constitutes the virus. Easier said than done, of course.

As UNICEF (2020) reminds us, "only 3 out of 5 people worldwide have basic handwashing facilities." The UNICEF Fact Sheet (2020) makes for sobering reading: 900 million school children are unable to wash their hands because the schools they go to do not have enough water. It is important to note that these startling statistics haven't shown up only in the context of the COVID-19 outbreak. At the best of times, water is taken for granted by most people in privileged settings; yet, as WHO (2019) points out, "785 million people lack even a basic drinking-water service" and "at least 2 billion people use a drinking water source contaminated with faeces." Unpacking these figures reveals how women and girls face specific social, cultural, and structural forms of discrimination in their access to safe water and sanitation, with gender interlocking with ethnicity, caste, religion, disability, and other factors in shaping the power dynamics around water allocation and rights (see, e.g., UNESCO, 2019).

Inequities around the access to water and the fight for even a semblance of parity can be seen in the struggles over water played out across the globe – over water privatization, damming of rivers, and the destruction of waterways by the extractivist industry. Almost all of these struggles are, not surprisingly, located on the lands of marginalized communities and Indigenous territories, and subaltern publics everywhere have taken the lead in forging alliances to claim their rights. In this chapter, we focus on two very different campaigns of resistance, one against the privatization of water, including the commercial bottling of the vital resource of water, and the other against corporate and state attempts to prioritize oil extraction and transportation over protecting water resources sacred to Indigenous people. In each case, an alternative pathway of public relations cuts through the concrete walls of corporate public relations.

Message in a bottle

The insidious trend of commodifying water is manifested most prominently in the bottling of drinking water, an industry promoted relentlessly by the corporate communication machinery. The bottled water market is estimated to be galloping at a compound annual growth rate of "around 13.5 % over the forecast time frame 2018–2026" and is tipped to reach a "valuation of US\$ 217.12 billion by 2026" (MarketWatch, 2019). This phenomenal growth has paid huge dividends for shareholders of corporations selling a resource vital for human survival as a product in the marketplace. Promotional strategies lure the well-heeled global consumer public to pay for something that people should have a right to access, with images of "pure fantasy" – "pictures of mountains, streams and pristine nature" that spring forth nutrient and mineral-rich water (Leonard, 2010). This is despite the fact that much of the bottled water actually comes from a public source. Pepsi's Aquafina and Coca-Cola's Dasani brands of water, among others, are, for example, drawn from public sources (Byron, 2007), although both companies claim to subject the water collected to purification processes. The water is packaged not just in single-use plastic bottles but also in a seductive good-health narrative for elite publics. The packaged message by the money-spinning bottled water industry bypasses publics at the lower end of the hierarchy who have little or no access to clean drinking water. The branding of bottled water rests on semantic massaging, and the claims made by some of the big corporations marketing their bottled water defy the limits of realistic assessment. For example, as Pacheco-Vega (2019) says:

> in Mexico a Gerber-branded bottled water promotes itself as "water especially created for your baby" (in Spanish: www.nestle.com.mx/ brands/agua-gerber). Unless Nestlé has managed to create a different type of hydrogen and oxygen combination that is especially suited for babies (and even then, populations are wildly diverse, different and heterogeneous), it is hard to believe that the way in which Gerber bottled water is branded can even be legally used. However, it is, as shown by the market share captured by Nestlé globally, and in Mexico. In France,

Perrier brands itself as "an iconic French brand." Perrier harnesses the power of French identity to position itself as the brand for an entire country.

(p. 10)

Furthermore, the International Bottled Water Association (IBWA) and the Beverage Marketing Corporation announced in a media release that "Bottled water has become consumers' No. 1 drink" and that this reflected "a clear trend of consumers increasingly choosing safe, healthy, convenient, zero-calorie bottled water" (IBWA, 2017). Each of the adjectives "safe, healthy, convenient, zero-calorie" used in the media release is targeted to global middle-class consumers looking for safe and healthy beverage options. The IBWA (n.d.) website, for example, declares that

> to lead a healthier life, one of the simplest changes you can make is drinking water instead of other beverages that are heavy with sugar and calories. So, if you want to eliminate or moderate calories, sugar, caffeine, artificial flavors or colors, and other ingredients from your diet, choosing water is a right decision.

Such messaging resonates with affluent members of the public who resort to what Szasz (2007) calls an "inverted quarantine" where people consume products such as bottled water to insulate themselves from environmental harms – a contrast from the public health model of quarantine where the focus is to protect the public from a contagion. In an "inverted quarantine," there is little interest in changing the underlying causes of the problem. Instead, as Szasz (cited in McNulty, 2008) says, "Consumers believe these products will protect them, which creates a kind of political 'anesthesia' that severely reduces their willingness to participate in collective political action to generate real change."

Alongside emphasizing the importance of shifting away from sugary drinks is the increasing attention of water corporates to demonstrate their green credentials. By depicting bottled water as being sourced from pristine springs or snow-clad mountain works, corporations "attach signifiers of sustainable consumption" to their products but hide their "unsustainable business models" in mining and processing their products (Andersen, 2015, pp. 411–412). As Andersen (2015) says, "corporate green branding, with its influx of cash, leaves conservation efforts divided, the public misled, and an unsustainable culture of consumption largely intact" (p. 413).

While corporations focus on appealing to their most desired publics – consumers – they have also found a way to cater to the next rung of the hierarchy of publics (Munshi & Kurian, 2005), namely, Western environmental activists. Citing the example of "Dow Chemical's 'The Future We Create' campaign [featuring] images of clear water in multiple hues of blue," Andersen (2015, p. 412) talks about how the corporation co-opted water activists and NGOs by inviting them to participate in the Future of Water virtual conference as a part of its campaign. While the IBWA (n.d.) maintains that "the bottled water industry is a strong supporter of our environment and our natural resources," Nestlé's (2017) "Pure Life Begins Now" campaign focuses on "our wider commitment to reduce our environmental impact, as all bottles can be recycled." Faced with a growing movement against plastic use, some of the big water companies are planning to do away with bottles altogether, instead concentrating on setting up commercial water fountains that dispense water for a fee (Maloney, 2019). The high-end water brand Flow, endorsed by actress-turned-entrepreneur Gwyneth Paltrow's wellness and lifestyle company Goop, is said to be "changing the game with a spring water that is naturally alkaline – nothing added – in 100% recyclable packaging. The pack is made from sustainably sourced fibers and even has a plant-based cap crafted from sugarcane" (Beer, 2019).

At the same time, there has been a dramatic shift towards bottled or packaged 'sachet' water in Third World countries where public access to clean drinking water has become increasingly limited for vast swaths of the population. Pacheco-Vega (2019) points out that "Water insecurity is particularly acute in cities as infrastructures are substantially sensitive to exogenous shocks, including extreme climatic events, accelerating urbanization and explosive population growth" (p. 1). The abdication of responsibility by central and local authorities to ensure public access to safe drinking water in countries as diverse as Mexico, Niger, and India, compounded very often with their complicity with (or capture by) corporate interests, has meant that individual consumers have been left to fend for themselves in their efforts to avoid contaminated tap water (see, e.g., Pacheco-Vega, 2019; Keough & Youngstedt, 2018), even though the cost of bottled water puts it out of reach of the most deprived sections of society. Indeed, given the gender-based division of labour across much of the developing world, where women are responsible for providing food and water for the household (see, e.g., Bhavnani, et al., 2016; Kurian, 2000), it is in the urban context of slums and informal settlements that we find some of the most significant unequal gender impacts of water privatization (see, e.g., Sultana, Mohanty, & Miraglia, 2013). Ironically, it is often the case that bottled and sachet water offer no guarantee of safer water, given the possibilities of plastic leaching into water, chemical toxins, or even pathogens (CSE, n.d.; Keough & Youngstedt, 2018). The problem of contaminated water, of course, is not confined to the Third

World. Whether it is in the predominantly impoverished African American community of Flint, Michigan, in the US which were exposed to toxic lead in their drinking water (Ranganathan, 2016; Pulido, 2016), or in rural communities such as Havelock North in New Zealand which were struck by a campylobacter outbreak (Radio New Zealand, 2017), access to safe drinking water is not only a function of class, gender, and race but also of the neoliberal economic order that seeks profits before all else.

The public relations of water revolving around the packaging of neatly crafted messages on health and happiness gained from bottled water does not acknowledge the publics that barely have a foothold on the lowest rungs of the hierarchical ladder. These publics constitute over 2.2 billion people on the planet who do not have access to safe drinking water at home (Ritter, 2019), people struggling to cope with the intensifying global crisis of freshwater, marked by scarcity, pollution, and depletion of ground water (Barlow, 2007). In this context, the idea of "water wars" (Shiva, 2002) takes on fresh credence, evidenced not so much in wars between states but rather in the struggles over control of water resources involving states, corporations, and people on the ground.

If those who live Nestlé's Pure Life are publics at one end of the spectrum, Indigenous populations in different parts of the world are often at the other end. Shimo (2018), for example, records the story of a mother of five, Iokarenhtha Thomas, and her family, who live in the Six Nations of the Grand River Indigenous reserve in Ontario, Canada, with no access to running tap water while "Nestlé extracts millions of litres of water daily from Six Nations treaty land." Similarly, Lopez and Jacobs (2018) report on the hardship faced by the residents of San Cristóbal de las Casas in Chiapas, Mexico, "where some neighborhoods have running water just a few times a week" but a "Coca-Cola factory on the edge of town" has "permits to extract more than 300,000 gallons of water a day as part of a decades-old deal with the federal government." In New Zealand, over 23 billion litres of water a year for bottling and export is being extracted by private corporations for a cost of as little as $200 a year in the context of widespread drought conditions, despite widespread Māori and public opposition (Dreaver, 2019; MacLennan, 2020). For example,

> In Whakatāne, Ngāti Awa and Sustainable Otakiri have been fighting back against a foreign company's plans to expand existing water bottling at Otakiri Springs by up to 1.1 billion litres a year. In 2018, Nongfu Spring subsidiary Creswell NZ Ltd was granted consent to increase the water taken by 27,400%, with the goal of drawing 208,000 litres every hour of every day by 2021.
>
> (MacLennan, 2020)

Opposition to such water bottling endeavours is grounded in concerns that they violate Māori rights to water, enshrined in the Treaty of Waitangi signed between the British Crown and over 500 local Māori chiefs in 1840 (see, e.g., New Zealand Law Society, 2019), as well as the recognition that they contribute to plastic pollution, while the profits from sales of a precious resource accrue exclusively to foreign companies with no benefit to New Zealand.

Against the obvious imbalance of power among stakeholders, long-marginalized publics are rallying together and forging chains of solidarity communicatively. Struggles against the corporatization of water and inequitable access to this life resource are beginning to resist the agenda set by dominant elites. The acts of resistance are palpable even in the face of violent suppression, such as the murder of Indigenous activists in Honduras and Brazil, often coordinated by a nexus of corporations, the military, and the state (Pearce, 2017). We now explore the ways in which an alternative set of public relations is at play with disparate yet inextricably linked movements around the world making their voices heard as they seek to reclaim their rights to water by weaving together concerns for cultural identity, social sustainability, and environmental justice in new enactments of sustainable citizenship.

Against the tide but with the flow

Citizenship anchored by sustainability goes beyond the binaries of "rights and obligations; territorial and non-territorial conceptions of citizenship; the public and private arenas as possible sites of citizenship activity; and competing virtue- and non-virtue based ideas of citizenship" (Dobson, 2003, p. 37). One of the core tenets of sustainable citizenship is therefore not only to make sense of polarized views on issues of social, cultural, economic, and environmental importance but also to negotiate dialectical tensions inherent in the discourses around such issues. The discursive pulls and pressures on these issues are captured in the dialectics of, for example, "rights and responsibilities, state and non-state, public and private, human and non-human nature, universal and particular, and democracy and capitalism" (Kurian et al., 2014, p. 437). In articulating the need for a fair and equitable share of water for all living creatures, subaltern publics around the world are exercising their right to redefine what water stands for by engaging with these dialectics. For example, water movements have problematized the idea of rights, exposing at the same time the collusion between states and corporations that blurs the perceived lines between the state and non-state and between the private and the public. In 2010, the United Nations General Assembly and the Human Rights Council recognized "the human right to water and sanitation" (UNDESA [United Nations Department of Economic and Social Affairs], 2014). This was a landmark step towards making sure that people had access to water no matter where they lived and what their socio-economic status was. But the UN resolution placed the onus of fulfilling this right upon "states and international organisations," requiring them "to provide financial resources, help capacity-building and technology transfer to help countries" for clean water and sanitation (UNDESA, 2014). As with all other rights, it has been up to states in the first instance to make the right to water real for their citizens, but most have failed the vulnerable segments of their population. The poor and Indigenous communities in both developed and developing countries, communities we refer to as subaltern publics, have the least access to clean drinking water.

The neoliberal economic world order, in which international financial institutions wield considerable influence over states because of their conditional lending policies (Babb & Kentikelenis, 2018), creates a context where states look to prioritize economic growth and profitable ventures over citizens' needs and rights. In the case of Flint, Michigan, for example, it was "the shrewd, neoliberal language of fiscal austerity" that was used to justify cuts to "infrastructural costs by switching its residents to toxic water in 2014" (Ranganathan, 2016, p. 27). Alongside deregulating economic activities and limiting social services, this context also encourages the privatization of natural resources (Stiglitz, 2002). Margaret Thatcher's sweeping neoliberal policies led to the privatization of water utilities in all of England and Wales in 1989 (Bakker, 2001). In subsequent years, as the World Bank and the International Monetary Fund (IMF) invoked the condition of privatization into their lending contracts for developing nations, countries across South America and Africa were pushed to open up water supply arrangements to the private sector (Barlow & Clarke, 2002; IATP, 2002).

The most talked about location of such privatization was Bolivia, which also saw the most successful act of resistance against the move. In an incisive critique, Bhavnani and Bywater (2009) write about the devastating consequences of the Bolivian government's contract with Aquas del Tunari, a consortium of corporations that included a subsidiary of Bechtel, and the concurrent passing of Law 2029, a pro-privatization law, under the influence of the World Bank. The huge rise in water costs for the people, often up to 300% (Olivera, 2004), and the deprivation of a life source for the poor, led to a massive resistance movement by the *La Coordinadora de Defensa del Agua y de la Vida* (The Coalition in Defense of Water and Life), coordinated, for the most part, by women (Bhavnani & Bywater, 2009). The protests, which ultimately forced the Bolivian government to withdraw the contract, broke the state-corporation nexus and set the stage for resistance movements around the world against the narrative of economic profitability and service efficiency, in order to establish water as a human right that ought not to be priced out of the reach of the poor.

The success of the Bolivian movement is an example of sustainable citizenship in action. As Dwinell and Olivera (2014) point out, it was not merely a resistance to privatization but "a popular struggle to expand participation in determining the conditions of people's lives," with the "Coordinadora's base of power" being "grounded in people autonomously deliberating, deciding upon, and implementing the decisions of the people" (p. 47). These decisions went beyond what the state could, or would, do:

> The boycott of the water bills and the breaking of the contract with Aguas del Tunari were not possible within the confines of the state – they *were* illegal – but that is what the people chose to do and that is what was done.
>
> (Dwinell & Olivera, 2014, p. 48)

The Bolivian movement has had significant influence on Latin America. In Uruguay, for example, a campaign in 2004 led by "civil society groups, trade unions and the left-wing Broad Front coalition" for a referendum resulted in reforming the constitution to make access to piped water and sanitation services a human right (Ortiz, 2011). In Peru, Ecuador, and Chile, communities have risen up to protest against water shortages in areas where elites control water resources, and water movements have become part of wider struggles for equity and access (Vidal, 2017). Water protection movements launched by local farmers, Indigenous people, and women have also been successful elsewhere – for example, the closure of a Coca-Cola factory in Plachimada, Kerala, where the corporation was extracting 500,000 litres of water a day, leading to environmental pollution from toxic sludge. The alliances of resistance movements in the Global South led to the Plachimada Declaration at an international conference in Plachimada in 2004, which proclaimed that "water is not a private property, not a commodity" but rather a common resource and a fundamental right (*The Hindu*, 2004). A sustained resistance movement against water privatization by Solidaritas Perempuan, a diverse group of women workers in Jakarta, Indonesia, also led to a legal victory against the state as well as a number of corporations in 2017 (Arun Kumar, 2018).

More recently, local concerns about water bottling, especially by Nestlé in the US and Canada, has led to a series of grassroots campaigns (Jaffee & Case, 2018), while in New Zealand, similar concerns have resulted in Māori/iwi and environmental activists opposing efforts to extract water from resources that are subject to Māori treaty claims (Radio New Zealand, 2020). Campaigners in North America were able to lobby government officials and create broader public support for their cause by using the droughts of 2012 and 2016 to highlight issues of scarcity and equity and linking these issues to climate change, "eventually winning concessions in their battle with Nestlé" (Jaffee & Case, 2018, p. 497).

Each of the campaigns, characterized by mobilization and resistance, is illustrative of sustainable citizenship at work. According to the Rapid Transition Alliance (2019), resistance movements have led to at least 235 cases of 'remunicipalization,' or a return of water to public control, spread across 37 countries between 2000 and 2015. These movements demonstrate, as Sultana (2018) points out, "water's connection to broader issues of democracy, citizenship and development" (p. 487). Picking up on Sultana's (2018) assertion that "water justice is never only local, but cross-scalar and global" (p. 487), we argue that the struggles against the neoliberal agenda of commodifying water represent the efforts of building solidarity among subaltern publics across geographical boundaries.

As Fletcher, van Heelsum, and Roggeband (2018) say, "conflicts over water privatization are conflicts over hegemony" and there is a need for a "a coherent counter-hegemonic agenda" (p. 241). The resistance movements have a long way to go yet, but the public relations of sustainable citizenship provides a vehicle for shaping the counter-hegemonic agenda required to change the narrative on water.

Oil and water do not mix

One of the most powerful instances of violent conflicts in recent times between a corporate agenda of profiteering through oil extraction and Indigenous determination to protect culturally sacred water and lands is seen in the case of the Dakota Access Pipeline (DAPL) (Estes, 2016; Whyte, 2017; Privott, 2019; Proulx & Crane, 2020). The DAPL is an 1800-km (1,172-mile) pipeline that carries over 500,000 barrels of crude oil a day from oil fields in Bakken, North Dakota, to oil refineries in Illinois in the US, crossing four states, going under the Missouri River, and snaking through the sacred lands of the Lakota, Dakota, and Nakota peoples of the Oceti Sakowin (the Great Sioux Nation). The DAPL story is one of ongoing colonization and forcible alienation of land and water from Indigenous people that began in the mid-19th century (for a concise historical overview of this period, see Estes, 2016). The long history of broken treaties that marked the relationship between the US and Indigenous nations paved the way for a takeover of millions of acres of land and of rivers that were culturally, spiritually, and economically vital, through the promotion of incentives such as gold mining and farming to potential settlers. The active promotion of settler colonialism, defined by Whyte (2017) as "a type of injustice driven by settlers' desire, conscious and tacit, to erase Indigenous peoples" (p. 159), led to a systematic campaign of dismantling the long-established complex societies of the Lakota and Dakota nations and their "Indigenous govern-ance systems that support cultural integrity, economic vitality, and political self-determination and the capacity to shift and adjust to the dynamics of ecosystems" (Whyte, 2017, p. 160).

The 1851 Treaty of Fort Laramie, renegotiated in 1868, created the Great Sioux Reservation, which guaranteed that the Sioux could live there "permanently" and comprised "most of contemporary South Dakota and parts of North Dakota, Montana, Wyoming, Nebraska, and Colorado" (Proulx & Crane, 2020, p. 51). As was the case with treaties signed by colonial powers elsewhere in the world, the US Congress was quick to override the provisions of this treaty. In 1889, the Great Sioux Reserva-tion was split into six separate reservations, and the ensuing resistance by the Indigenous people was violently suppressed at Wounded Knee Creek in 1890 when 300 Lakota people were massacred. Equally signifi-cant was the struggle over control of the Missouri River. According to Estes (2016), in the early 20th century, the desire of the Missouri River basin states to create large dams for irrigation was thwarted by a 1908 Supreme Court ruling that the "tribes maintained access and control of water within original treaty territory." But this was bypassed with the passing of the Flood Control Act in 1944 and the subsequent building of five dams, "which targeted and disproportionately destroyed Native lands and lives" (Estes, 2016).

As a classic example of the corporate trend of constructing what Wer-nick (1991) called "promotional cultures," the Texas-based oil company that constructed the DAPL, Energy Transfer Partners (ETP), runs a dedi-cated website, called the "Dakota Access Pipeline," showcasing the pipe-line's technical safety, its economic contributions, and its environmental benefits – all to serve the interests of the nation. Celebrating its role in trans-porting "light sweet crude oil," ETP lists the many benefits of the DAPL, including:

> [G]reater energy security, lower trade deficit, and boosted economic growth ... approximately 8,000 to 12,000 jobs during construction ... [and] paying millions in property taxes to states each year, [which are] used to support schools, hospitals, emergency services and other critical ongoing needs.

It also pronounces its ability to deliver all of this while fully comply-ing and even exceeding obligations to consult Indigenous people in the Standing Rock Reservation. The company's effort to use corporate public relations tools to show itself as a community citizen is clearly geared towards elite publics:

> The threat the project posed to the tribal peoples, who are on the margins of society, remained invisible in the corporate communication space. Strategic communication thus drives capitalistic corporate practices along a development agenda but, overtly or covertly, does so at the expense of the interests of vulnerable segments of the population.
>
> (Munshi & Pal, 2018, p. 2)

As critical scholars of promotional cultures say, corporations often put "communication to work," and in such a process their goal of public communication is not necessarily "to circulate vital information, reach reasoned ('rational-critical') consensus, or ensure democratic participation" but instead to "provide settings for presentation, promotion, and persuasion, with the ultimate goal of economic advantage" (Aronczyk & Powers, 2010, p. 9 and p. 13). We can see the act of putting communication to work on the ETP's website, where it says that the DAPL "is not a threat to the Tribe's water supply or cultural sites" and that it crosses the Missouri River 70 miles from the new water supply source for the tribe:

> This Dakota Access Pipeline crosses almost entirely private land, often already in use for other utility easements. The pipeline does not cross the Standing Rock Sioux reservation, even at the portion of the pipeline that was the subject of dispute at Lake Oahe. In developing the route, the United States Army Corps of Engineers had hundreds of contacts with dozens of tribes regarding the Dakota Access project. In addition, the U.S. Army Corps reached out to the Standing Rock Sioux Tribe nearly a dozen times to discuss archaeological and other surveys conducted before finalizing the Dakota Access route.

Such statements seek to "silence or make invisible Indigenous claims both about the land from which they are or could be displaced and about the consequences of national development projects for their lives and identities" (Proulx & Crane, 2020, p. 52). They suppress the reality of the historical context of illegal colonial dispossession of land and water that were never ceded by the Sioux. The overwhelming emphasis on the sanctity of 'private property' and 'legal process' serves two purposes in their communication to dominant publics (including their shareholders, the state, and 'mainstream' society) – one, they attempt to legitimize corporate profiteering by demonstrating that building the DAPL is within the law (and ignoring that what is legal is not necessarily ethical); and two, they attempt to delegitimize

Indigenous people's actions challenging the DAPL as being outside the boundaries of law. In contrast, the subaltern publics of the Standing Rock Sioux nation and their allies articulate an embodied, materially and spiritually grounded vision of life that is dramatically distinct from those who champion the DAPL.

The construction of the pipeline, centred around Lake Oahe near the Standing Rock Reservation in North Dakota, was rejected by the Standing Rock Sioux Tribe in December 2015 (Privott, 2019). But when their objections to the DAPL were ignored by the US Army Corps of Engineers (ACE), it led to a broad-based movement, #NoDAPL, with a sophisticated use of social media, led initially by Indigenous youth that spread to include Indigenous women and men, and non-Indigenous allies from around the country and beyond. In April 2016, members of the Standing Rock youth group, including 13-year-olds Anna Lee Rain Yellowhammer and Tokata Iron Eyes, created a change.org petition to stop the DAPL. Emphasizing the centrality of water to all life, they said: "In Dakota/Lakota we say 'mni Wiconi.' Water is life. Native American people know that water is the first medicine not just for us, but for all human beings living on this earth" (Yellowhammer & Iron Eyes, 2016).

> The teenagers' petition was the cornerstone of the Standing Rock Youth's #ReZpectOurWater campaign. Expertly navigating Twitter, Instagram, Facebook and YouTube to elevate their voices and those of others at Standing Rock, the young people's petition spread across social media with the #NoDAPL, #ReZpectOurWater and #StandWithStandingRock hashtags.
>
> (Petronzio, 2016)

Refusing to accept the juggernaut of the corporate- and state-backed DAPL as inevitable, the youth group mobilized itself (Elbein, 2017). It organized spiritual relay runs, educated the public through teach-ins, created videos, wrote letters, and set up camps on tribal land "to get their message out and to remind the broader public that the United States is still, and has always been, Indigenous land" (Dhillon, 2016). It was the transformative work of the youth and Indigenous women as water protectors that catalyzed what is considered to be the largest Indigenous movement on the continent.

A central strand of the #NoDAPL movement was the work of these water protectors who drew on "an ethos of responsibility" in their work encompassing "responsive care in/to the interconnectedness of life, the special role of women in the care of water, and the collective survival of Indigenous women in colonial and patriarchal violence" (Privott, 2019, p. 74). Even as the youth leaders were launching their efforts, in April 2016, the first water protection camp, the Sacred Stone Camp, was erected on the ancestral land of Lakota historian and activist LaDonna Bravebull Allard (Allard, 2016). "The water protectors successfully worked, prayed, and strategized to catapult this movement into mainstream settler-colonial and global discourse through sharing their message of *protection*, not protest" (Privott, 2019, p. 75). Quoting Northern Arapaho writer Misty Perkins, Privott (2019) says that "the central difference between protection and protest is that water protectors are not protesting in a land dispute but 'protecting the land and waters against its very destruction for ALL OF US, for ALL life'" (p. 75). In a sense, this also illustrates the difference between protest public relations (Adi, 2019) and public relations as sustainable citizenship. The latter is about resistance to dominant, often colonizing, forms of promotion in a way that safeguards the resources of the earth for all its people, especially those who are unrepresented by formal organizations.

Thus, against the message of universal economic benefits, national energy security, environmental protection, and the legitimacy of constructing the DAPL offered by ETP and the state, the subaltern publics – the Indigenous people and their allies – offer a radically different vision of the world. It is a vision that recognizes a shared responsibility to protect the earth:

> As Native people, being connected with Mother Earth and the Great Spirit, we have great connection with everything around us. The trees, the grass, the plants, even the rocks . . . and without that water, we're nothing, because we're made of water too.
> (Tingling Star Woman, cited in Privott, 2019, p. 81)

This worldview of the interconnectedness of Indigenous people and water is seen in their rallying cry "Mni Wiconi" (water is life) and the recognition that "We are the river, and the river is us. We have no choice but to stand up" (Allard, 2016). This message of interconnectedness, sharpened by the resistance to ongoing colonization, has resonated globally, drawing in support from environmental justice organizations, women's organizations, and civil rights organizations (see, e.g., Steinman, 2019). The public relations as sustainable citizenship of the water protection campaigns is evident as the resistance to the DAPL shows "the convergence of solidarity from across the continent," effectively promoting "an articulation of environmental justice and Indigenous sovereignty as intersecting concerns" (Proulx & Crane, 2020, p. 61).

The solidarity these campaigns garnered included those from formally constituted organizations, helping build relationships with activist groups in the process. Greenpeace, for example, consulted Indigenous activists on the ground in opposing the DAPL and undertook a range of actions 'behind the scenes' to support the water protectors (Molina, 2016). This included helping "Indigenous People's Power Project (IP3) lead non-violent direct action trainings at the camps, where they trained more than 400 people in how to take peaceful, meaningful direct action to stop the pipeline" (Molina, 2016), supporting petitions to put pressure on President Obama, and donating "supplies to help water protectors stay at camp through the harsh North Dakota winter" (Molina, 2016). Another powerful voice raised in support of the #NoDAPL movement was that of Black Lives Matter (BLM). Janaya Khan, co-founder of BLM Toronto, led a delegation to Standing Rock, stating, "We were invited, and, by the grace of the creator, we're here channeling Black Lives Matter on indigenous land, following indigenous and native leadership" (*Democracy Now*, 2016).

The relationship building among activists and minority communities is an expression of public relations that is inherently political and stands for social justice. It challenges and resists the mainstream public relations-crafted narrative of water as a marketable commodity and shows how "water is essentially about power," a kind of power that "is intersectionally experienced by gender, class, race, and other axes of social difference" (Sultana, 2018, p. 485). It is a profound betrayal of the trust vested in the state to fulfil its responsibility of looking after the most vulnerable segments of a country's population, as it is often a perpetrator of aggression against these segments through the policies it enacts. For example, construction of public utility projects by the state on Indigenous territories lead to Indigenous communities losing access to their land and their traditional water sources on the land (Misiedjan & Gupta, 2014).

The public relations of subaltern communities in their struggles over water engages with the dialectics of the state and the non-state as it seeks to focus on the "broader connections that tie peoples, places, policies and ecologies in far-flung places" (Sultana, 2018, p. 485), often catalyzing non-state organizations to counter the state-corporation nexus in promoting the inherently inequitable ideology of the market. Both cases discussed in this chapter also illuminate the dialectical tensions between rights and responsibilities at multiple levels – individual, community, state, and corporations – as well as between democracy and capitalism. In the Indigenous recognition of their oneness with water, we also see a fundamental questioning of the human-non-human divide. But, more than anything else, we see how disparate movements, straddling the Global North and the South, are building networks of solidarity by fighting for the principle of water as a commons:

> Social justice and human rights groups, local communities, small farmers, peasants and indigenous peoples fighting to maintain traditional control over their lands, and a growing movement around the world to

stop the privatization of areas once considered the common heritage of humanity, all promote this view.

(Barlow, 2010, p. 184)

In the next chapter, we move to terra firma as we take a critical look at the unabashed promotional culture of discourses that justify the control over land and the emotionally powerful resistance to such discourses.

4 Land

Changing the narratives of occupation and imposed identities

Four decades ago, the Palestinian-American cultural critic Edward Said had eloquently described the sophisticated ways in which colonial powers justified their dominance over their colonies through art, architecture, and literature. As Said's (1978) seminal work *Orientalism* documents, the colonizer's expansionist plans rested around communicating a discourse of superiority, a superiority that could justify grabbing other peoples' lands in the name of what the French colonizers called the *mission civilisatrice*, or the civilizing mission for the English. Although Europe was just another part of the world, indeed much smaller (and demographically younger) than Asia, Africa, or the Americas, it cultivated a communication strategy to show itself as larger than life to make its conquests seem righteous (Chakrabarty, 2008).

Daniel Defoe's (1719/2014) *Robinson Crusoe*, Robert Louis Stevenson's (1882/2001) *Treasure Island*, George Henty's (1884/2017) *By Sheer Pluck: A Tale of the Ashanti War*, and H. Rider Haggard's (1885/2007) *King Solomon's Mines* are just a few of the numerous examples from fiction of the expression of colonial superiority. Similarly, colonial powers routinely used advertising and other communicative means to exercise their hegemony: "Advertising took scenes of empire into every corner of the home, stamping images of colonial conquest on soapboxes, matchboxes, biscuit tins, whiskey bottles, tea tins and chocolate bars" (McClintock, 1995, p. 507).

Yet, postcolonial literature and literary criticism have provided us with a narrative of resistance. Works such as Chinua Achebe's (1964) *Arrow of God*, Chimamanda Adichie's (2006) *Half of a Yellow Sun*, Amitav Ghosh's (2008) *Sea of Poppies*, Patricia Grace's (1986) *Potiki*, Jamaica Kincaid's (1988) *A Small Place*, Jean Rhys's (1966) *Wide Sargasso Sea*, and Ngũgĩ wa Thiong'o's (1967) *A Grain of Wheat* express the voices of the people of formerly colonized or settled lands such as Nigeria, India, Aotearoa/New Zealand, Antigua, Jamaica, and Kenya in their own contexts and against the canon.

A focus on the actions of subaltern publics

In addition to anti-colonial literary figures, subaltern historiographers (see Chapter 1) presenting history through the eyes of the colonized have inspired a group of scholars (e.g., Dutta & Pal, 2010, 2011; Munshi & Kurian, 2005, 2007) to centre resistance in communication. These scholars have challenged the dominant narrative of public relations scholarship and its obsession with elite publics by re-focusing attention on the tools of resistance used by less-known characters and publics in "alternative histories of communicative action that remain largely un-documented" in mainstream literature (Munshi & Kurian, 2016, p. 407). For example, Munshi, Kurian, and Xifra (2017), in their search for "(an)other story" (p. 366) of public relations embedded in the works of postcolonial novelists, show "how colonized peoples used their own forms of public relations to resist colonialist practices and rally subaltern publics together" (p. 366). The characters in each of these works are ordinary folk, marginalized by the colonial apparatus, who band together to communicate their struggles over land and identity.

These postcolonial novels are in a sense a public relations of sustainable citizenship as they communicate a discourse that can speak for the subaltern, a discourse that actively *resists* the discourse of colonialism. If "colonialism" is, as Munshi, Broadfoot, and Hall (2017) say, "not merely a material expression of power through military interventions or through economic policies exercised by rich states and corporates to control poorer entities, but is essentially a *discourse* of hegemonic control and domination" (p. 1887), the most effective way of challenging it is by attempting to change the discourse. For example, Dutta and Pal (2010) talk about the acts of resistance by the Zapatista National Army to free trade agreements in Mexico, and the struggles by Indigenous groups against colonialist attempts to exploit their long-held natural resources in Peru. It is important to document the actions of subaltern publics who "seek to transform the oppressive global structures through globally-connected networks of global solidarities" (Dutta & Pal, 2010, p. 365) because it "is in these spaces of resistive practices that alternative imaginations of public relations as a field of engagement that imagines the possibilities of structural transformation . . . can become possible" (Dutta & Pal, 2011, p. 205).

Communicating to problematize power, challenge dominant publics and the discourses they marshal, and reclaim identities lost in territorial colonization is at the heart of sustainable citizenship articulated in Chapter 1. It is in this context that we look at the communicative dimensions of discursive struggles on and over land manifested in an alternative conception of public relations exercised by publics marginalized by dominant narratives.

There are many examples of such struggles spread across the world in contemporary times, two of which we pay specific attention to for the sake of brevity and a sharp focus. These are the Boycott, Divestment, Sanctions (BDS) movement led by the supporters of Palestinians opposing the illegal occupation by the Israeli state of the parts of land mandated to them by the UN, and the resistance against state attempts to equate citizenship with religious affiliation in India.

Who drew the map of the land?

The story of the Middle East (or more accurately West Asia) is dominated by the conflict in Israel-Palestine and the changing contours of the maps of the region brought about by continuing dispossession of land by powerful publics. The rival claims to the 'holy land' notwithstanding, the state of Israel was created on the platform of a strategically planned and executed public relations campaign by Zionist activists (see, e.g., Toledano & McKie, 2013). In their insightful work, Toledano and McKie (2013) outline how Zionists achieved their objective "to persuade world public opinion to support Zionist goals" and "to raise resources for the implementation of the Zionist ideology and political plan" (p. 42). In keeping with the hierarchies of mainstream PR, the Zionist public relations machinery strategically ignored the major public of the Arab population who lived in Ottoman Palestine, a strategy that several "Israeli leaders still believe in" (Toledano & McKie, 2013, p. 44). It is hardly surprising therefore that Israel has been relentlessly occupying more and more of the UN-mandated Palestinian land through unauthorized settlements in the West Bank; cornering the bulk of the resources, including water; erecting walls to separate the people of the land; blockading the Gaza strip; and inflicting disproportionate aggression on Palestinians in the name of security (Fisk, 2005; Peled, 2013; Said, 2003; Veracini, 2006). The most influential sponsor of this ongoing PR offensive has been the US, which has consistently provided financial and military aid to Israel and has steadfastly blocked UN resolutions against the state (Chomsky, 2010; Mearsheimer & Walt, 2007). Mearsheimer and Walt (2007) describe in detail the PR strategies used by the "Israel lobby" in the US whose "political power is important not because it affects what presidential candidates say during a campaign but because it has a significant influence on American foreign policy" (pp. 5–6). According to Mearsheimer and Walt (2007), "it is difficult to talk about the lobby's influence on American foreign policy" or indeed on shaping a dominant pro-Israel narrative "without being accused of anti-Semitism or labelled a self-hating Jew" (p. 9). The latter labelling is particularly pervasive as some of the leading critics of the state are either Israeli or Jewish. The prominent feminist scholar Judith Butler (2012), who is Jewish and critical of Israel's policies, says:

> For me, given the history from which I emerge, it is most important as a Jew to speak out against injustice and to struggle against all forms of racism. This does not make me into a self-hating Jew. It makes me into someone who wishes to affirm a Judaism that is not identified with state violence, and that is identified with a broad-based struggle for social justice.

The Holocaust and the genocide of the Jews by Nazi Germany remains one of the most horrific examples of human brutality ever, and the vulnerability of the Jewish population to threats to its security and identity are well documented. However, the conflation of the need to make amends for the horrors of the Holocaust with the campaign to give total control of land to Israel, a land to which the Palestinians have as much claim, is what makes the issue contentious. The unconditional support of the US for Israel's increased takeover of Palestinian land has led to a discourse that labels any criticism of Israel as anti-Semitism (Butler, 2003). Indeed, this kind of labelling is an example of what the postcolonial communication scholar Mohan Dutta (2014) calls "communicative inversions" which deploy "the rhetoric of open communication to accomplish objectives that in reality reflect closed communication." To open up the debate, there is a need for a narrative of resistance, something that peace activist Miko Peled (2013), son of a former Israeli general and a Zionist, builds so eloquently in *The General's Son: Journey of an Israeli in Palestine*: "Mine is the tale of an Israeli boy, a Zionist, who realized that his side of the story was not the only side" (p. 4). The other side of the story, according to Peled, has not been adequately told. In a blog post, Peled (n.d.) describes his homeland as one where

> half the population is governed by a radical Zionist regime that sees the struggle for control over the land as a zero sum game, and the other half of the population is governed by the security forces of this Zionist regime; one nation ruling over another while controlling of the land and its resources.

Despite the absence of a focused public relations campaign to present their story, the Palestinians have built alliances with Israeli Jewish and global human rights activists over decades and have begun to successfully reach out to the world with their narratives of persecution, loss, and desire for the return of their own land, a kind of public relations as resistance. An example of this is the Boycott, Divestment, Sanctions (BDS) global

movement. This organically growing movement campaigns for an economic and cultural boycott of institutions and businesses complicit in the
Israeli occupation of Palestinian land, divestment of investments in Israeli
companies that sustain the marginalization of Palestinians, and sanctions in
the form of banning of trade and other business arrangements with Israel
until it complies with international law (Barghouti, 2011; Bullimore, 2012).
The movement, started by Palestinian civil society in 2005, "allows people
of conscience to play an effective role in the Palestinian struggle for justice" (BDS movement, n.d.). This campaign, which has a long way to go, is
pushing against the far-more-entrenched Zionist narrative. It thus succeeds
in reaching out to a global citizenry, educating many about the everyday
brutal realities of Palestinians while providing an avenue to express solidarity with them. Munnayer (2014), for example, points out that the BDS
"is actually shifting attention *toward* the Palestinian plight. It is doing so
before new audiences, and in ways and places that were not imagined a
mere five years ago." Similarly, student-led initiatives, such as Students for
Justice in Palestine, which has a presence especially in universities in the
United States and Canada, are examples of local initiatives for education
and awareness-raising about the situation in Palestine while also promoting
the BDS movement.

In line with the contours of sustainable citizenship outlined in Chapter 1, the BDS movement has problematized the notion of power. It has
attempted to show that the Israel-Palestine conflict is not a simple case of
two competing narratives but one in which the Zionist narrative on ownership of the 'holy land' has wielded greater influence and that the first
step towards resisting this influence is to disrupt the mainstream discourse.
The BDS movement has three primary requirements, which ask that Israel
(1) should end "its occupation and colonization of all Arab lands occupied
in June 1967" and dismantle the illegal wall; (2) recognize the "fundamental rights of the Arab-Palestinian citizens of Israel to full equality"; and
(3) uphold the rights of "Palestinian refugees to return to their homes and
properties as stipulated in UN Resolution 194" (BDS movement, n.d.). In
a nuanced analysis, McMahon (2014) explains how each of the campaign's
three requirements "contests a discursive rule" (p. 77).

First, the emphasis on the words 'occupation' and 'colonization' disrupts
any notion of a discursive equality between the messages of the two parties. Unlike other discourses of conflict, the campaign shows that there
is no parity between the two sides of a dispute. The terms 'occupation'
and 'colonization' put the spotlight on the "profound power asymmetries"
between "settler-colonists and indigenous peoples," and "that people think
and speak of Palestinian-Israeli politics in terms of a relatively empow-
ered foreign party violently dispossessing a relatively disempowered

indigenous party" (McMahon, 2014, p. 77). Second, the call for Israel to "recognise the fundamental rights of its non-Jewish citizens" challenges Israel's "claimed unique identity as a homeland for religious exiles and the only 'modern democracy' in a region of Arab rejectionists" (McMahon, 2014, p. 77). Finally, the third call "to respect the rights of Palestinian refugees to return to their homes and properties in accordance with UN Resolution 194. . . violates the manner in which the discourse delimits the temporality of Palestinian-Israeli politics" and focuses on how the arrival of the Zionists "meant dispossession and dislocation for Palestinians" (McMahon, 2014, p. 78).

From a public relations perspective, therefore, the campaign has not only succeeded in showing the power imbalances in the narratives of the Israel-Palestine conflict but has also mobilized publics at the periphery of the conflict to exert pressure on a dominant state, expanding in the process the political public sphere around the conflict. For example, the Black Lives Matter movement, a campaign by the subaltern public of Black youths fighting against institutional discrimination in the US, endorsed the BDS in August 2019 in an act of solidarity. The campaign has also managed to equate the plight of Palestinians to those living under apartheid in once-segregated South Africa, a strategy that has succeeded in bringing together socially responsible organizations from around the world to rally in its support. As Thrall (2018) points out,

> in an era of corporate social responsibility, BDS has given bad publicity to major businesses tied up in Israel's occupation and helped push other large firms out of the West Bank. It has disrupted film festivals, concerts and exhibitions around the world. It has riled academic and sports organisations by politicising them, demanding that they take a stand on the highly divisive conflict.

In one sense, a marker of the success of the BDS movement is the backlash against it, not only from the Israeli state but also from states that support the dominant Zionist narrative. Israel has launched a counter offensive against organizations that support the BDS, and in the US, as Human Rights Watch (2019) points out, 27 states have passed laws to penalize those who call for or participate in boycotts against Israel. So jolted have Israel, its allies, and supporters of the Zionist narrative been by the BDS campaign's inroads into the public imagination that it has decreed the activities of the BDS supporters as 'anti-Semitic.' But, as discussed earlier, while anti-Semitism in any form is abhorrent and cannot be condoned, using the term to dismiss any criticism of the Israeli state is misplaced. Asserting that "the conflation of anti-Zionism with anti-Semitism is a bit of rhetorical sleight-of-hand that depends on treating Israel as the embodiment of the Jewish people everywhere," Goldberg (2018) says that "it's increasingly absurd to treat the Israeli state as a stand-in for Jews writ large, given the way the current Israeli government has aligned itself with far-right European movements that have anti-Semitic roots."

As a campaign, the BDS movement has been able to script a narrative of non-violent resistance to the Zionist discourse of occupying Palestinian land. Indeed, it has, as Thrall (2018) says, nudged the "Palestinians away from an anti-occupation struggle . . . towards an anti-apartheid one." Although comparisons with the pre-1994 apartheid South Africa are dismissed by some commentators (e.g., Pogrund, 2015), the description of the situation in Palestine by anti-apartheid icon and Nobel laureate Desmond Tutu does give credence to the BDS narrative. In writing about Barghouti's (2011) book on the BDS, Tutu (2011) says:

> I have been to Palestine where I've witnessed the racially segregated housing and the humiliation of Palestinians at military roadblocks. I can't help but remember the conditions we experienced in South Africa under apartheid. We could not have achieved our freedom without the help of people around the world using the nonviolent means of boycotts and divestment to compel governments and institutions to withdraw their support for the apartheid regime.

The endorsement of Tutu and several other influential peace leaders has galvanized an alternative public relations campaign which has led to networks of BDS proponents that "are diverse, multicultural, and concerned with a variety of social justice issues" (Hallward, 2013, p. 34). In line with our discussion of feminist notions of empowerment (Chapter 1), the BDS movement is also seen as an expression of feminist solidarity: it has

> provided feminists and other activists in Palestine, Israel, and worldwide with a clear vision and manifold opportunities to mobilize the international community to confront Israeli apartheid and to join the struggle to bring about a just and lasting resolution of the conflict.
>
> (Sharoni, 2012, p. 126)

In commenting on the support of the BDS by several feminist scholar members of the National Women's Studies Association (NWSA), Sharoni, a gender studies academic and a co-founder of Feminists for Justice in/for Palestine, says that "We're basically redefining feminism and putting solidarity with Palestine into that definition of what it means to be a feminist" (cited in Redden, 2015).

While focused on Palestinian rights to a specific area of contested land, the campaign negotiates the dialectical tensions of the particular and the universal by raising larger issues of equity, justice, and sovereignty in its narrative. The campaign is not geared to the organizational interests of any one activist group; rather, it is an exercise in relationship building among a diverse set of publics both inside Israel and in different parts of the world, underpinned by a message of resistance to colonizing attempts by the Israeli state to take over land far in excess of what was mandated to it by the UN.

Does land have a religion?

If the BDS movement is largely against the unjust occupation of Palestinian land, the struggles of minority communities in contemporary India are against the attempt by the current ruling regime to conflate land with religious identity and religious identity with national identity. Independent India was partitioned by the departing British colonial regime on religious lines into a Hindu-majority India and a Muslim-majority Pakistan in 1947 (Talbot & Singh, 2009), a move that was followed a year later by the setting up of Israel as a Jewish state in 1948 (Bregman, 2002). But while Israel proclaimed its Jewish identity (Bregman, 2002), India chose to remain secular from the beginning, although the word 'secular' was formally added to the Preamble of the Constitution only in 1976 (Forty Second Amendment, 1976). The country's secular pathway was deeply resented by right-wing outfits such as the Hindu Mahasabha and the Rashtriya Swayamsevak Sangh (RSS), a paramilitary, Hindu nationalist organization committed to a vision of India as a "divine object (the Hindu nation)" (Andersen & Damle, 1987, p. 76). The invocation of India's divinity in the form of a goddess of sorts has been the core of the RSS discourse of land as the "sacred geography where the nation resides" (Andersen & Damle, 1987, p. 77), a line it has taken to spread its divisive message of India as a land of Hindus. Within a year of India's independence, a Hindu extremist, Nathuram Godse, assassinated the 'father of the nation' and leader of the country's freedom movement, Mahatma Gandhi, a vocal proponent of inter-religious peace and harmony.

Since then, the RSS as well as several other organizations professing *Hindutva*, "an ideology of militant Hindu nationalism" (Snehi, 2003, p. 10), kept up both overt and covert campaigns to whip up hostilities against minorities, eventually leading to the ascent to political power of the Bharatiya Janata Party (BJP), a pro-Hindu party made up of cadres of the RSS and allied Hindutva forces. The BJP sowed the seeds of Hindu majoritarianism when it first came to power in 1998 and ruled until 2004.

However, it was in 2014 when the party returned to power under Narendra Modi, once an RSS *pracharak* (campaigner), that its unabashedly Hindu ideology began seeping into the state machinery, gaining momentum when the party was re-elected with an increased majority in 2019. This is when the state narrative took on a blatantly anti-Muslim turn, with the nation's 200 million Muslim citizens (the world's second-largest Muslim population) projected as an 'other.' In a particularly controversial step, the BJP-led government pushed through the Citizenship Amendment Act (CAA) in December 2019, allowing refugees from Hindu, Sikh, Buddhist, Jain, Parsi, or Christian – but not Muslim – communities from Afghanistan, Pakistan, or Bangladesh to gain Indian citizenship (Press Information Bureau, 2019).

On paper, the government has been trying to project a humanitarian image of itself by stepping forward to help minority communities facing persecution in neighbouring countries to get Indian citizenship. Prime Minister Modi was cited in *The Times of India* (2019) as saying that "the newly introduced CAA is meant to give refuge to the persecuted refugees" as he launched a social media campaign to promote it. Similarly, PTI (Press Trust of India) (2020a) reported Defence Minister Rajnath Singh declaring that "India had fulfilled" its "moral duty" towards religious minorities in Pakistan, Afghanistan, and Bangladesh who were in a "life of misery."

But the specific exclusion of Muslims is telling, especially because many Muslims of certain denominations also face persecution in the three countries chosen (see, e.g., Khan, 2003, for an analysis of the persecution of Ahmadiyyas in Pakistan). Besides, the neighbouring country of Myanmar, where the atrocities against the minority Muslim Rohingya community are well documented (United Nations Human Rights, 2018), has been excluded as a source country. It is when the CAA is looked at in conjunction with the setting up of a National Register of Citizens (NRC) that the anti-Muslim narrative and agenda of the state become most apparent. Home Minister Amit Shah's announcement in Parliament that the NRC (originally restricted to the border state of Assam) would be extended to all of India, a move projected to root out "illegal immigrants and infiltrators" (Joy, 2019), invoked fear among minority communities. The government has strenuously denied that the CAA was anti-Muslim, with Prime Minister Modi insisting that the "CAA is not going to take away anybody's citizenship" (Schultz, 2019). But if and when an NRC is in place, the onus will be on residents to provide documentary evidence of their ancestry to get on the NRC, a requirement with which many in the country, especially in villages, will struggle to comply. Again, the lack of documentary evidence will not disadvantage any community other than Muslims because the CAA would facilitate citizenship for Hindus and non-Muslim minorities even if they could not prove the Indian credentials of their parents: "Only document-less Muslims will face the prospect of detention centres, or being stripped of all citizenship rights" (Mander, 2019).

The term 'illegal immigrant' is an evocative one and part of jingoistic race and ethnicity-based narratives around the world that seek to protect the land from foreign settlers. The "nativist rhetoric – that immigrants are invading the homeland – has gained ever-greater traction" (Becker, 2019) and can be seen in anti-immigration political campaigns popularized by President Donald Trump in the US (Ledford, 2016; Demata, 2017) and by politicians in a range of states who use carefully crafted communication strategies to target visibly different immigrants (see, e.g., Hjerm & Bohman, 2014). In the context of the situation in India, however, the so-called nativist rhetoric is also directed against its own minority citizens.

Despite the notion of secularism being enshrined in the Indian Constitution and the constitutional rights of all people living in the country regardless of the faith they profess, the state under its current dispensation has relentlessly tried to communicatively construct India as a land of and for Hindus. Even the articulation of Hinduism in the state-sponsored narrative is a rather limited version of Hinduism, confined as it is to a monolithic, predominantly upper caste, framework of Hindu values, norms, and beliefs (Mankekar, 2015). This is despite the fact that Hindus themselves are ethnically and linguistically diverse and divided along caste lines, and they have not historically followed any uniform path (Ludden, 1996). Ironically, the Hindutva ideologues governing the country have borrowed the tools of the erstwhile colonial rulers in casting Hinduism as a dogmatic and singular religion along Judeo-Christian lines. As Thapar (1989) points out, "Orientalist scholarship" was "anxious to fit the 'Hindu' process into a comprehensible whole based on a known model" (p. 218). Like the Orientalists, the BJP has chosen to propagate a straitjacket version of Hinduism. One prime example is the way it has gone about opposing cow slaughter and the sale of beef. While many upper caste Hindus do not touch it, beef has been an important part of the diet for Dalits, groups historically repressed socially for being classified in the lowest rung of the caste system, as well as of non-Hindu communities. Cow vigilantism has been rising at an alarming rate in India, with radical cow protection groups, with the tacit support of the powers that be, killing people from minority communities often on the mere suspicion of consuming beef (Marlow, 2019). As Jain (2019) points out, "a similar symbolic language of the sacred cow was used in the early part of the nationalist movement to galvanize large numbers of Hindus across class, caste, and regional divides in British India," but what is strikingly different today is that the same language is being used by India's "ruling party members" against their own fellow citizens, "fanning and even supporting hatred against India's Muslims."

The cow-centred language of the Hindutva brigade is part of the BJP government's communication strategy of tying in its openly Hindu agenda with a faux nationalism and patriotism that is connected to a glorified image of India's Hindu past. However, as Bhatt (2001) argues, the ideology of Hindu nationalism being spread in contemporary India has much less to do with an ancient culture than with Western influences of the colonial era, including that of 1930s fascism, with the leaders of the RSS, such as Hedgewar, Savarkar, and Golwalkar, praising the actions of Hitler and Mussolini. So advanced is this fascism-influenced strategy that any criticism of the government's ideology or actions is conveniently branded as anti-national, or worse, pro-Pakistan. In India's most populous state, Uttar Pradesh, where Muslims have been bearing the brunt of a hardline Hindutva regime, a senior police officer was filmed asking people protesting against the CAA to "go to Pakistan" (Duncan, 2019). Similarly, a Delhi-based BJP politician called localities in Delhi protesting against the citizenship laws as "mini-Pakistans" and even described the impending elections as an "India Vs Pakistan clash" (Jacob, 2020). Even Prime Minister Modi used the Pakistan bogey when, at a public meeting, he called upon anti-CAA protesters to "expose Pakistan's deeds on the world stage" (PTI, 2020b). He went on to say:

> If you want to shout slogans, shout against the way in which atrocities are happening against minorities there; if you want to hold rallies, hold it in favour of Dalits and downtrodden who have come from Pakistan (to India). If you want to do *dharna*, do it against Pakistan's deeds.
>
> (PTI, 2020b)

As Saran (2020) says,

> The RSS-BJP combine has disfigured love of country into a red-eyed, pop-veined Hindu nationalism and diligently pretends that there is no difference between government and nation. If you criticise Modi, you're a traitor trying to break India (eyeroll), because you hate Hindus (eyeroll), and/or are being paid by Pakistan/China/The West (eyeroll).

The communication strategy of the dominant, Hindu-hardline state in today's India parallels that of corporate public relations in as much as it is targeted to maximizing the interests of elite publics, in this case politically and economically powerful Hindu blocs seeking to imprint their superiority on the social and economic frameworks of the nation. Banaji (2018) discusses the "consequences of an alliance between Hindutva communications, global neoliberal capitalism and an orientalist desire to recuperate a single high-caste version of Hinduism" (p. 335) and says:

> The insidious process of flooding the public sphere with images and signs of Hindu supremacy, of culling text books, and initiating Hindu supremacist schools, colleges and training camps has been joined by the faster and more agile processes of taking over boardrooms and media houses, running networks of trolls and normalising extreme violence. Thus, vigilante publics are created, while mobs, storm troopers and their mouthpieces in media and judiciary are supported by political allies adept at demonising liberal-secular discourse.
>
> (p. 346)

In essence, the dominant narrative of nationalism caters to the majority community in India by demonizing minority publics, most overtly Muslims but also intellectuals, secularists, students, or for that matter any constituency that has another, more inclusive vision for India. It also equates land with religion, demanding that anyone opposing the dominant narrative should go to Pakistan.

In this fraught context, publics marginalized by the dominant Hindutva discourse have embarked on a movement of resistance facing down the might of the state. An uncoordinated movement, bringing together a wide range of disparate groups of dissenters to the state's divisive policies, stands out as an exemplar of what public relations as sustainable citizenship looks like. Since the enactment of the CAA in December 2019, subaltern publics of students and ordinary citizens have taken to the streets, lanes, and public spaces to resist the unconstitutional and discriminatory nature of the CAA and the NRC. This resistance is not led by any political party but by groups committed to the idea of justice and the secular goals of the Indian Constitution. In fact, in a piece written on the occasion of India's Republic Day on 26 January 2020, Saran (2020) writes: "Indians are putting the 'public' back into 'republic.'"

If, as we say in Chapter 1, "the notion of sustainable citizenship encompasses building active relationships among a variety of publics" to empower those without power, the anti-CAA challenges in India have managed to do just that. The protests are not led by specific activist groups; rather they are often spontaneous acts of resistance across the country by students and scholars, men, women, transgender people, community organizations, and workers coming together to fight a state machinery marshalling pliant police and other security forces. These groups have been unfazed by the use of brutal state force to break up protests, most notably at Jamia Millia Islamia University in Delhi and Aligarh Muslim University on

15 December 2019 (Gaur, 2019; Mathur, 2019; Kuchay, 2019). Eminent historian Irfan Habib was quoted by the PTI (2019) as saying that the public sentiment against the CAA expressed a struggle for the "idea of India as a modern state" and that the police action against protesters "has been worse than in colonial times."

Given that the colonial rulers were masters of brutality, the massacre of 400 unarmed civilians at Jallianwala Bagh in the Punjab city of Amritsar by Brigadier-General Reginald Dyer's imperial troops in 1919 being one of many sordid examples, the question is not so much whether the present-day police action against protesters is worse than in colonial times. Rather, the point is that the current action is justified on the basis of a shaky notion of nationalism. It is this flawed idea of nationalism that the protesters are out to dismantle with their counter-narrative.

If Jallianwala Bagh was a flash point for the freedom movement against British rule, Shaheen Bagh became a rallying point for resistance groups in contemporary India in late 2019 and early 2020. The low-profile locality in South Delhi was one of the most visible faces of the anti-CAA protests, with the protesters helping "us understand resistance as an expression of belonging and citizenship as a participatory tool, rather than a status granted by the state on the basis of select documents" (Farooqi, 2020, p. 13). The protesters at Shaheen Bagh were new to expressing dissent publicly and came from everyday walks of life:

> Some of them are students, some are matriarchs. There are young women with small children in their laps. There are great-grandmothers. There are artists and organizers, poets and singers. Sometimes they are angry, other times they laugh with abandon. They take time off to pray, to go home and keep the kitchens functional. They return with determination.
>
> (Badhwar, 2020)

From a communication standpoint, there are similarities of the actions of those sitting on the road at Shaheen Bagh with what might be seen as actions of protest public relations (Adi, 2019), especially in the way they took to getting their counter-narrative out in performative ways. However, although there were activists in their midst, as a group, they did not seem to adopt any planned strategy normally associated with activist public relations:

> Speakers and performers come and leave the stage, knowing very well that the actual performance, a hearteningly interminable one, is before them and not by them . . . there are students and activists who are found

running initiatives to inform people through creative art, doing sessions with children on harmony, peace, and compassionate living, inculcating mindfulness through conversations, and so on. None of these people are to be found on the stage or in the audience. A protest that goes beyond the immediate visible site of reference suggests deep connections that exist between resistance and belonging.

(Farooqi, 2020, p. 14)

The marginalized publics of Shaheen Bagh, as also those elsewhere in the country, resisted the narrative spun by Hindutva ideologues on who constituted as legitimate claimants to the land. In the true essence of citizenship, these minority publics succeeded in deploying the state's own symbols of nationhood and pride in their messages of resistance. For example, every gathering had the Indian national flag fluttering, people read passages from the Indian Constitution and paid homage to leaders of the country's freedom movement. On Republic Day (26 January), as also on New Year's Day, those at the gatherings sang the national anthem, a 'protest song' that Carnatic music maestro and social activist T. M. Krishna calls "the spirit of incredible possibility, the idea of India, human struggle, and much more" (quoted by PTI, 2020c). The spontaneous gatherings of resistance in different parts of the country eventually stopped after the government imposed a nationwide lockdown to prevent the spread of the COVID-19 virus, but the message of the acts of resistance still resonates.

In seeking to cast its citizens as one monolithic public and base its public relations strategy to target this public, the current Indian state seems to ignore the many publics that make up the diverse country. As Mackey (1998) says, "nationalist narratives do not . . . represent the actual lived and multiple sentiments" of nations "cross-cut by region, language, race, gender, class and culture" (p. 151). Such narratives undermine people's rights to the land of their birth by using what Mackey (1998) calls "discursive devices" that seek to subsume multiple identities under one majoritarian identity. Those challenging the dominant narrative provide a living template for sustainable citizenship by problematizing power, expanding the political public sphere, breaking down hierarchies of publics, and resisting dominant narratives and channels of communication. That women have been at the forefront of the resistance movements against the citizenship laws in India is not surprising. As Kurian (2020) says, these women

fully embrace the idea that women's freedom means little if other groups are still oppressed. With its economic critique, disavowal of caste oppression and solidarity across religious divides, India's Shaheen Bagh sit-in shares attributes with the women's uprisings in Chile, Lebanon, Hong Kong and beyond.

The resistance also confronts the dialectics of the state and the non-state by showing how a state that has the duty to protect all its citizens explicitly privileges some citizens over others and how those portrayed by the state as anti-national resist by actively invoking the national constitution. Further, public relations as a process of resistance in the Indian case, as in the Israel-Palestine case, disrupts the easy conflation of religion (or, for that matter, any sectarian identity) and nationhood and legitimate claims to land. There are some similarities between the long-running resistance movements in the Middle East and the more recent resistance movements in India. While the former is against a state founded on a religion-based platform, the latter is against a state that is attempting to change its inherently secular nature to a majority religion-based one.

Whose land is it anyway?

Land has been a site of contestation from ancient times with wars fought over its possession, boundaries marked around ownership and tenancy, and ever-changing conflicts and negotiations over access and use of resources on it. It has been the site of domination and resistance, colonization and freedom movements. Land is the material foundation for discourses around notions of citizenship defined by nationhood, place of birth, immigration and emigration, and other territorial conceptions, all of which too often privilege elite segments of society. Such limited ideas of citizenship are propped up by exclusionary ideologies spun by majoritarian groups, as evident in the cases of Israel and India discussed in this chapter, to entrench their hegemonic control over land. If, as Monbiot (2020) says, "politics is best understood as public relations for particular interests," the governing political machineries in these two nations (as indeed in many others) use public relations to promote the interests of dominant publics in maintaining control over land and its resources. The public relations of citizens resisting such interests, on the other hand, sees citizenship as a cultural idea encompassing the "lived experience" of people (Williams, 1960) that bring together "values, beliefs, customs, traditions, symbols, norms and institutions" to "create the overarching frames that shape how humans perceive reality" (Assadourian, 2015, p. 98). Such an alternative form of public relations advances the idea of sustainable citizenship not only by engaging with the dialectics of the state and non-state, rights and responsibilities, and religious identity and nation, but also by problematizing the concepts of land

and borders and citizenship based on passports, residency, and spurious allegiances to flag posts of power. It also emphasizes the telling of powerful stories of resistance regardless of whether the objectives of the resistance are met or not. The actions of resistance themselves constitute a public relations of sustainable citizenship.

5   Earth
Public relations for the planet and its people

Strategic communications industries and practices have continued from colonial times until now to abet the efforts of "states, institutions, and corporations to legitimize undemocratic practices in the name of development" by providing them with "a medium to privilege the meaning of land as property over the cultural meaning of land as sacred" (Munshi & Pal, 2018, p. 2). Although, at a material level, land conquests and the subjugation of the people living on the land are the most visible signs of colonization, the communicative aspects of domination can also be seen in the realms of water and air. Corporate public relations efforts, for example, to justify the privatization of water resources, and to find ways to keep the wheels of consumption rolling despite the threats of climate change, are indeed a part of the neo-colonial communication apparatus. All such public relations narratives, crafted in line with the neoliberal logic of free-market capitalism and the primacy of private enterprise, are processes of covert domination and exploitation (Munshi & Kurian, 2005, 2007; Dutta & Pal, 2011). Such manufactured narratives have obscured the core meanings of air, water, and land as sources of life and sustenance on Planet Earth and markers of identity for the people who inhabit it, especially marginalized communities around the world.

Spaces of resistance

An alternative lens of public relations, however, also reveals spaces of resistance where 'other' publics have contested dominant narratives, found discursive and material spaces to disrupt colonial and neo-colonial capitalism, and challenged assumptions that the earth is there for the taking (see, e.g., Dutta, 2012; Dutta & Pal, 2011; Jefferess, 2008; Munshi & Kurian, 2016; Roy, 2004). In recognizing that spaces where communities marginalized by existing dominant structures speak up are spaces of potential transformation, our spotlight on communicative acts of resistance illuminates a radically different idea of public relations, one that is delinked from organizations or specific interests but is geared towards what we call sustainable citizenship. Conceptualizing public relations in this way not only exposes and highlights the self-interested, self-absorbed, manipulative, and unethical characteristics that give mainstream public relations a disreputable label but also gives us a map of the trajectories public relations does take as actions of resistance and could potentially take in challenging injustice in a variety of political, economic, social, environmental, and cultural contexts. Such a public relations – one as sustainable citizenship – is made up of the inter-connected, inter-woven networks of relationships and alliances that revolve around the Earth-centred values and principles of equity, justice, inclusion, creativity, compassion, and love.

Each of the cases we provide in this book, covering the realms of air, water, and land, critiques the approach of mainstream public relations that works to serve elite corporate and/or state interests and provides an account of the resistance to this dominant approach by publics that are outside the line of vision of public relations' dominant managerial frame. In the chapter on air, we expose the ways in which key extractivist industries and colluding states use their public relations machinery to, overtly or covertly, prevent action on climate change, by far the biggest threat facing the planet. At the same time, the chapter shows how climate movements led by the subaltern publics of Indigenous peoples and youth are building alliances of solidarity to challenge the hegemony of corporate and political elites and save the planet from imminent catastrophe. Similarly, the chapter on water focuses on the powerful linkages initiated by Indigenous communities with non-elite publics to challenge the dominant economic narrative of the DAPL in the Standing Rock Reservation in the US and of the privatization of water worldwide, shifting attention, in the process, to Indigenous rights, equity, and justice. Finally, in the chapter on land, we highlight the efforts of subaltern publics in the Israel-Palestine region and in India to challenge the material, oppressive, and essentially divisive state narratives that are sugar-coated by specious narratives of majoritarian nationalism deployed by ruling political regimes.

There are several insights to be gleaned from the cases discussed in this book. One is how entrenched the hierarchy of publics still is in mainstream public relations. Narratives of what is rather euphemistically referred to as the 'development project' surround land grabs for industrial development, construction of dams and pipelines, drilling and fracking for oil, and logging of trees in tribal lands by states and corporations around the world. The cases highlighted in this book, as well as many others, illustrate how contemporary predatory capitalism rides on public relations campaigns, spearheaded by political and economic super-elites everywhere who neglect publics not seen to be formal stakeholders. For example, Indigenous publics are rarely represented in the flamboyant communication plans drawn up by corporates and states alike to further 'development,' a legacy of the colonial project. Colonization, and its descendant, neo-colonization, have erased "Indigenous peoples' adaptive capacity and self-determination by repeatedly containing them in different ways, destroying the ecological conditions that are tightly coupled with Indigenous cultural and political systems" (Whyte, 2017, p. 94).

A second insight is that the struggles of the Indigenous people call into question the current global world system predicated on state sovereignty. Indigenous peoples have never wilfully ceded sovereignty in the first place. Colonial acts of semantic jugglery in asserting sovereignty over colonized lands are evident, for example, in Aotearoa/New Zealand in the context of the Treaty of Waitangi. The English version of the Treaty of Waitangi noted that the chiefs had acceded to the Crown "all the rights and powers of sovereignty" over the territories, while the Māori version (called Te Tiriti o Waitangi) clearly states that the chiefs gave the Crown "te Kawanatanga katoa" – understood by Māori as the governance of the land (Orange, 1987/2010, p. 31). This difference in the two versions of the treaty is significant because the Māori believe that the authority given to the Crown to govern in return for protection never amounted to the ceding of sovereignty. Of course, in many other parts of the world, colonial powers did not even bother about the niceties of written treaties and simply asserted their rights based on the might of their military power. Today's struggles over land and water continue what began from the time of first contact.

Given this context of domination of Indigenous rights and identities by colonizing forces in the name of the state, much of the resistance to the neo-colonial narratives of development rests on tearing down the assumptions of absolute state sovereignty. The cross-national alliances of Indigenous and non-Indigenous peoples in the struggle against state-supported corporate predatory interests demonstrate how the sovereignty of the state can be challenged. As evident in the cases across the domains of air, water, and land, the state tends to follow dominant ideas couched in misrepresented principles of democracy: political elites aligning with corporations in stakeholder engagement exercises that gloss over the needs of marginalized communities on the impacts of climate change; state enterprises actively joining water privatization initiatives even when access to basic water resources elude the poor; and governments treating electoral successes to indulge in a tyranny of the majority. Perhaps it is in the struggles over land – in Israel-Palestine and in India – that we see most clearly the coercive, violent power of the state to dehumanize, delegitimize, and systematically destroy those publics it deems expendable to its task of realizing its vision of the ideal 'imagined' national community (Anderson, 1983).

Linked to the second insight is a third one – that a notion of public relations that rests on principles of justice and equity needs to problematize the idea of the state and facilitate the building of relationships that transcend the state. Referring to Thomas Piketty's (2014) advocacy for a global wealth tax, Noisecat (2016) says that levying such a tax would need an international governance structure and notes how Piketty "pushes us to think beyond the state." Noisecat (2016) goes on to say that on a similar plane, "Indigenous demands for lands, jurisdiction, and sovereignty imply that we must think beneath it."

Looking 'beyond' and 'beneath' the state calls for grappling with the dialectics of the state and non-state. In the cases of climate change, water privatization, the DAPL, and the land, place, and identity-focused conflicts in Israel-Palestine and India, we see the state exercising its sovereignty to privilege the few over the many. In the cases of climate change and water, the sovereign state functions as a handmaiden to national and global corporate power, abdicating its responsibilities of care and wellbeing of its citizenry to facilitate the expropriation of resources by those who control the neoliberal economic order. In the process, states see subaltern publics – the Indigenous, the youth, the poor, and marginalized women, for example – as the unwanted and undesired 'other,' who are deemed superfluous to the project of development and modernization. Yet, the subaltern publics are not voiceless victims; in every case, we see the power of the alliances built in the transnational, national, and local contexts of the 'non-state.' The dialectical tensions between the state and non-state and between democracy and capitalism are among the many such tensions the framework of sustainable citizenship addresses. Such a framework "does not focus on compromises; rather it seeks to neutralize issues of power by concentrating not on 'gains and losses' but on the dialectical nature of the issues which are neither black nor white but have several shades of gray" (Kurian et al., 2014, p. 437).

The rise of promotional cultures that has characterized the forces of globalization and free-market capitalism is premised on the illusion of public relations, advertising, and lobbying thriving in democratic societies (Davis, 2013). A fourth insight of our book echoes Gray's (2009) observation that, very often, "democracy and the free market are rivals, not allies" (p. 17) as democratic aspirations of citizens are thwarted by market imperatives brought to bear upon them (Kurian et al., 2014). But, at the same time, as we have shown, subaltern publics reclaim the state, breathe life into the notion of democracy, and contest the unfettered power of neoliberal capitalism through their powerful, creative, and often subversive messages of resistive action. Water is a pivotal point of confrontation in the tensions between democracy and capitalism, bringing to the fore ongoing struggles against colonization and neo-colonialism. Around the world, struggles over control of water have pitted the Indigenous, women and men in local communities, water activists, and freshwater scientists, among others, against the commodification of water. In the process, the public relations strategies of the corporates – emphasizing health, safety, purity, and even the human right to water – are pitted against the envisioning of water by subaltern publics as inseparable from humanity and belonging to all. In seeing water as part of who they are, the women water protectors of the Sioux nation also reveal the dialectical tensions between the human and the non-human. Indigenous peoples around the world have never shared the Western worldview of nature as something to be owned, bought, and sold. The Māori in New Zealand, for example, trace their whakapapa (genealogy) to the mountains and the rivers that constitute the land of which they are a part.

The ability of the women water protectors to portray resistance through the idea of 'protection' rather than 'protest' is a striking feature of public relations as sustainable citizenship in Chapter 3. In contrast, in the cases of climate action (Chapter 2) and the struggles over land and identity (Chapter 4), protests and other forms of actions become a means of protection – of the climate, of identity, and claims of belonging. Indeed, a major insight from the cases covered is the leadership of women in every action of resistance, ranging from the work of women working on climate action in climate-ravaged countries (Chapter 2); the women leading the anti-water privatization struggles from Bolivia and Indonesia to Canada and the US (Chapter 3); and the women at the forefront of Delhi's Shaheen Bagh resistance against the discriminatory citizenship laws in India (Chapter 4). The varied experiences of women on "the front lines of resistance" (Bhavnani et al., 2016) tell an alternative story of social change against market-driven ideologies and forms of oppression in a variety of contexts. From a public relations of sustainable citizenship point of view, the cases show how the actions of resistance took the focus away from specific actors but brought women and men together in the struggles for social change. As Bhavnani et al. (2016) say,

> it is not by, for, or about women alone; in trying to better understand women's lives in all the glorious messiness of resistance and subordination, we realize more clearly that feminist futures are about men as well.
>
> (p. xxiii)

A final insight is that public relations is not, or should not, be seen merely as an activity focused on narrow organizational interests, whether corporate or activist ones, orchestrated by *actors* who strategically deploy communication to manage their own interests or resist others' interests. There is another kind of public relations – one that serves as sustainable citizenship – that is built around *actions* of resistance that interrogate power, form alliances among publics fighting for justice and equity, and, in the process, provide representation to those unrepresented. These actions may be invisible from the perspective of mainstream public relations as were the actions of the peasants in colonial histories of India that Guha (1983) talked about. But re-casting public relations and decolonizing the method-ologies of research in the field in ways that allow the counter-narratives of resistance, as envisaged by Smith (2012) in Indigenous studies, gives us an opportunity to re-imagine public relations as a vehicle of resistance. All of these insights are wrapped around the frame of power, politics, and solidar-ity that holds together our alternative idea of public relations as a form of communicative action of resistance. Drawing as we do on Arendt's (1970, 1972) notion of power as the capacity to act with others and on feminist notions of collective empowerment, we open up the potential for public relations to be a process of building solidarity to resist forms of injustice.

This kind of public relations certainly draws inspiration from activist public relations but is not limited to activism. Nor does it consciously use strategies and tactics associated with mainstream public relations. Instead it disrupts the mainstream public relations strategies of dominant political and economic interests by addressing dialectical tensions of engaging with the complexity of power as it is lived and enacted in a global, neo-colonial, and capitalist context.

Afterword

We started writing this book at our home institution of the University of Waikato in New Zealand, advanced the manuscript during our sabbatical at the London School of Economics and Political Science (LSE) in the United Kingdom, and put the finishing touches to it during a period of self-isolation in New Zealand, when much of the world was under lockdown to prevent the spread of COVID-19. The global panic and chaos around the advance of a disease with no vaccine, closing of borders, cancellation of public trans-port, the freefall of economic structures, the collapse of tourism, and the exposure of the huge gaps between the haves and have-nots, brought home to us more strongly than ever before the need for communication structures framed around sustainable citizenship.

The public relations of capitalism and neoliberalism have relentlessly promoted the illusory charms of private enterprise and the seductions of choice that come with it, undermining public institutions and the collabora-tive spirit of the commons. The huge reliance on public health in free-market economies at the time of the crisis of COVID-19 has exposed the limits of privatization and the promotional cultures associated with it. At the other end of the spectrum, states have used the crisis to drive people into shells of nationalism, closing their borders to outsiders and making vulnerable segments of the population perch on barbed wires of fragile lives and identities. This is a moment to recognize another kind of public relations. One that represents the unrepresented, one that challenges power implicit in the hierarchy of publics, one that builds solidarity by collaborating with a range of voices, one that puts the wellbeing of the planet and its inhabitants ahead of elite interests.

References

Achebe, C. (1964). *Arrow of god*. London: Heinemann.

Adi, A. (2019). Protest public relations: Communicating dissent and activism – An introduction. In A. Adi (Ed.), *Protest public relations: Communicating dissent and activism* (pp. 1–11). London: Routledge.

Adichie, C. (2006). *Half of a yellow sun*. New York: Knopf and Anchor.

Agarwal, A., & Narain, S. (1991). *Global warming in an unequal world: A case of environmental colonialism*. New Delhi: Centre for Science and Environment.

Allard, L. B. (2016, September 3). Why the founder of Standing Rock Sioux Camp can't forget the Whitestone massacre. *Yes!* Retrieved from https://tinyurl.com/ya9mjnhs

Allen, A. (1999). Solidarity after identity politics: Hannah Arendt and the power of feminist theory. *Philosophy and Social Criticism*, *25*(1), 97–118.

Allen, A. (2016). Feminist perspectives on power. In E. N. Zalta (Ed.), *The Stanford encyclopedia of philosophy*. Retrieved from https://tinyurl.com/yc96fnzd

Andersen, R. (2015). The "crying Indian," corporations, and environmentalism: A half-century of struggle over environmental messaging. In M. P. McAllister & E. West (Eds.), *The Routledge companion to advertising and promotional culture* (pp. 403–419). London: Routledge.

Andersen, W., & Damle, S. (1987). *The brotherhood in saffron: The Rashtriya Swayamsevak Sangh and Hindu Revivalism*. New York: Avalon Publishing.

Anderson, B. (1983). *Imagined communities: Reflections on the origin and spread of nationalism*. London: Verso.

Arendt, H. (1958). *The human condition*. Chicago, IL: University of Chicago Press.

Arendt, H. (1970). *On violence*. New York: Harcourt Brace & Co.

Arendt, H. (1972). *Crises of the republic*. San Diego, CA: Harcourt Brace Jovanocich.

Aronczyk, M., & Powers, D. (2010). Blowing up the brand. In M. Aronczyk & D. Powers (Eds.), *Blowing up the brand: Critical perspectives on promotional culture* (pp. 1–28). New York: Peter Lang.

Arun Kumar, B. (2018, August 2). *In Jakarta, a women's movement leads the fight against water privatization*. Retrieved from https://tinyurl.com/y9gpmrn6

Assadourian, E. (2015). Consequences of consumerism. In S. Nicholson & P. Wapner (Eds.), *Global environmental politics: From person to planet* (pp. 97–105). Boulder: Paradim Publishers.

Atmadja, S., & Verchot, L. (2011). A review of the state of research, policies and strategies in addressing leakage from reducing emissions from deforestation and forest degradation (REDD+). *Mitigation and Adaptation Strategies for Global Change, 17*(3), 311–336.

Babb, S., & Kentikelenis, A. (2018). International financial institutions as agents of neoliberalism. In D. Cahill, M. Cooper, M. Kronigs, & D. Primrose (Eds.), *The Sage handbook of neoliberalism* (pp. 16–27). Thousand Oaks, CA: Sage.

Badhwar, N. (2020, January 17). Speaking truth to power, in Shaheen Bagh and beyond. *LiveMint*. Retrieved from https://tinyurl.com/sjneca4

Bailey, R. (2018, February 7). Public relations as reputation management. *PR Academy*. Retrieved from https://tinyurl.com/y79pgk7c

Bakker, K. (2001). Paying for water: Water pricing and equity in England and Wales. *Transactions of the Institute of British Geographers, 26*(2), 143–164.

Banaji, S. (2018). Vigilante publics: Orientalism, modernity and Hindutva fascism in India. *Javnost – The Public, 25*(4), 333–350.

Bardhan, N., & Weaver, C. K. (2011). *Public relations in global cultural contexts: Multi-paradigmatic approaches.* New York: Routledge.

Barghouti, O. (2011). *Boycott, divestment, sanctions: The global struggle for Palestinian rights.* Chicago, IL: Haymarket Books

Barlow, M. (2007). *Blue covenant: The global water crisis and the fight for the right to water.* Toronto: McClelland & Stewart.

Barlow, M. (2010). The growing movement to protect the global water commons. *Brown Journal of World Affairs, 17*(1).

Barlow, C., & Clarke, T. (2002). *Blue gold: The fight to stop the corporate theft of the world's water.* New York: The New Press.

Baxter, L., & Scharp, K. (2016). Dialectical tensions in relationships. In C. Berger & M. Roloff (Eds.), *The international encyclopedia of interpersonal communication* (pp. 1–5). Hoboken, NJ: John Wiley & Sons.

BDS Movement (n.d.). What is BDS? Retrieved from https://bdsmovement.net/what-is-bds

Becker, J. (2019, August 10). The global machine behind the rise of far right nationalism. *New York Times*. Retrieved from https://tinyurl.com/y2taex3v

Beer, J. (2019, July 23). Bottled water's next trick is to make the bottle disappear. *Fast Company*. Retrieved from https://tinyurl.com/y8ss8bxd

Bell, A. (2020, February 14). Beware oil execs in environmentalists' clothing. *The Guardian*, pp. 181–195. Retrieved from https://tinyurl.com/tyq29du

Berger, B., & Reber, B. (2005). *Gaining influence in public relations: The role of resistance in practice.* Mahwah, NJ: Lawrence Erlbaum.

Beverley, J. (1994). Writing in reverse: On the project of the Latin American subaltern studies group. *Dispositio/n, XIX*(46), 271–288.

Bhavnani, K.-K., & Bywater, K. (2009). Dancing on the edge: Women, culture, and a passion for change. In K.-K. Bhavnani, J. Foran, P. Kurian, & D. Munshi (Eds.), *On the edges of development: Cultural interventions.* New York: Routledge.

Bhavnani, K.-K., Foran, J., Kurian, P., & Munshi, D. (2016). Preface to the second edition. In K.-K. Bhavnani, J. Foran, P. Kurian, & D. Munshi (Eds.), *Feminist futures: Reimagining women, culture, and development* (pp. xx–xxvi). London: Zed Books.

Bhavnani, K.-K., Foran, J., Kurian, P., & Munshi, D. (Eds.). (2019). *Climate futures: Reimagining global climate justice*. London: Zed Books.

Bhatt, C. (2001). *Hindu nationalism: Origins, ideologies and modern myths*. Oxford: Berg.

Böhm, S. (2013, April 12). Why are carbon markets failing? *The Guardian*. Retrieved from https://tinyurl.com/y7258euu

Bond, P. (2012). *Politics of climate justice*. Pietermaritzburg: University of KwaZulu-Natal Press.

Boykoff, M. T., & Boykoff, J. M. (2004). Balance as bias: Global warming and the US prestige press. *Global Environmental Change, 14*, 125–136.

Bregman, A. (2002). *A history of Israel*. London: Red Globe Press.

British Museum. (2020). *The BP exhibition/troy: Myth and reality*. Retrieved from https://tinyurl.com/yb2qdwue

Broom, G. M., & Dozier, D. M. (1986). Advancement for public relations role models. *Public Relations Review, 12*, 37–56.

Brown, A. (2019, December 14). How the fossil fuel industry is attempting to buy the global youth climate movement. *The Intercept*. Retrieved from https://tinyurl.com/ycka3s5z

Bullimore, K. (2012). BDS and the struggle for a free Palestine. In A. Lowenstein & J. Sparrow (Eds.), *Left turn: Political essays for the new left* (pp. 196–210). Melbourne: Melbourne University Press.

Butler, J. (2003). No, it's not anti-semitic. *London Review of Books, 25*(16), 19–21.

Butler, J. (2012, August 27). Judith Butler responds to attack: 'I affirm a Judaism that is not associated with state violence.' The war of ideas in the Middle East. *Mondoweiss*. Retrieved from https://tinyurl.com/yd9ys7pd

Byron, K. (2007, July 27). Pepsi says Aquafina is tap water. *CNN Money*. Retrieved from https://money.cnn.com/2007/07/27/news/companies/pepsi_coke/

Carrington, D. (2020, January 24). "Hypocrisy": 90% of UK–Africa summit's energy deals were in fossil fuels. *The Guardian*. Retrieved from https://tinyurl.com/tgfyby5

Centre for Science and Environment (n.d.). *Pesticides in soft drinks*. Retrieved from www.cseindia.org/pesticides-in-soft-drinks-1158

Chakrabarty, D. (2008). *Provincializing Europe: Postcolonial thought and historical difference*. Princeton, NJ: Princeton University Press.

Chandra, U. (2015). Rethinking subaltern resistance. *Journal of Contemporary Asia, 45*(4), 563–573.

Chandrasekhar, A. (2019, December 21). The UN climate talks ended in deadlock: Is this really the best the world can manage? *The Guardian*. Retrieved from https://tinyurl.com/ubhhdo6

Chomsky, N. (2010, August 16). The real reasons the U.S. enables Israeli crimes and atrocities. Interview with Kathleen Wells in Race-Talk, *AlterNet*. Retrieved from https://tinyurl.com/o6vgzrg

Climate Strike (n.d.). *It's time for a climate strike*. Retrieved from www.climatestrike.net/

Cook, J., Nuccitelli, D., Green, S. A., Richardson, M., Winkler, B., Painting, R., . . . Skuce, A. (2013). Quantifying the consensus on anthropogenic global warming in the scientific literature. *Environmental Research Letters, 8*(2), 24024.

Cook, J., Supran, G., Lewandowsky, S., Oreskes, N., & Maibach, E. (2019). *America misled: How the fossil fuel industry deliberately misled Americans about climate change.* Fairfax, VA: George Mason University Center for Climate Change Communication. Retrieved from www.climatechangecommunication. org/america-misled/

Coombs, W. T., & Holladay, S. J. (2012). Fringe public relations: How activism moves critical PR toward the mainstream. *Public Relations Review, 38*(5), 880–887.

Coombs, W. T., & Holladay, S. J. (2014). *It's not just PR: Public relations in society* (2nd ed.). Malden, MA: Wiley-Blackwell.

Cox, L. (2020, January 13). A billion animals: Some of the species most at risk from Australia's bushfire crisis. *The Guardian.* Retrieved from https://tinyurl.com/y8cu2jaf

Cretney, R., & Nissen, S. (2019, November). Climate politics ten years from Copenhagen: Activism, emergencies, and possibilities. *Women Talking Politics,* 16–19.

Cronin, A. M. (2018). *Public relations capitalism.* Cham, Switzerland: Palgrave Macmillan.

Crutzen, P. J., & Stoermer, E. F. (2000). The 'Anthropocene.' *Global Change Newsletter, 41,* 17–18. Retrieved from https://tinyurl.com/mlcvfzr

Cullis-Suzuki, S. (1992). *Severn Cullis-Suzuki at Rio Summit 1992.* Retrieved from www.youtube.com/watch?v=oJJGuIZVfLM

Curnow, J., & Helferty, A. (2019, December 20). A year of resistance: How youth protests shaped the discussion on climate change. *The Conversation.* Retrieved from https://tinyurl.com/y7k35dnp

Curtin, P. (2016). Exploring articulation in internal activism and public relations theory: A case study. *Journal of Public Relations Research, 28*(1), 1–16.

Curtin, P., & Gaither, T. K. (2007). *International public relations: Negotiating identity, culture, and power.* Thousand Oaks, CA: Sage.

Cutlip, S. M., Center, A. H., & Broom, G. M. (2000). *Effective public relations* (8th ed.). Upper Saddle River, NJ: Prentice Hall.

Davis, A. (2013). *Promotional cultures: The rise and spread of advertising, public relations, marketing, and branding.* Cambridge, UK: Polity Press.

Defoe, D. (1719/2014). *Robinson Crusoe.* New York: Open Road Integrated Media.

Delmas, M., & Burbano, V. (2011). The drivers of greenwashing. *California Management Review, 54*(1), 64–87.

Demata, M. (2017). "A great and beautiful wall": Donald Trump's populist discourse on immigration. *Journal of Language Aggression and Conflict, 5*(2), 274–294.

Demetrious, K. (2013). *Public relations, activism, and social change: Speaking Up.* London: Routledge.

Democracy Now (2011). "Get it done": After stirring Durban speech, student Anjali Appadurai initially banned by U.N. in Doha. Retrieved from https://tinyurl.com/y8xr394d

Democracy Now (2016). Black Lives Matter Delegation Returns from Standing Rock Camp (30 August). Retrieved from https://www.democracynow.org/2016/8/30/headlines/black_lives_matter_delegation_returns_from_standing_rock_protest

d'Entreves, M. P. (2019). Hannah Arendt. In E. Zalta (Ed.), *The Stanford encyclopedia of philosophy*. Stanford, CA: Metaphysics Research Lab, Stanford University. Retrieved from https://plato.stanford.edu/entries/arendt/

DeShazo, J. L., Pandey, C. L., & Smith, Z. A. (2016). *Why REDD will fail*. New York: Routledge.

Dhillon, J. (2016, June 20). Indigenous youth are building a climate justice movement by targeting colonialism. *Truthout*. Retrieved from https://tinyurl.com/y7t69ufw

Dobson, A. (2003). *Citizenship and the environment*. Oxford: Oxford University Press.

Down to Earth. (2011, December 3). AOSIS ultimatum to BASIC. Retrieved from www.downtoearth.org.in/news/climate-change/aosis-ultimatum-to-basic-68206

Dreaver, C. (2019, June 18). Government investigates royalty on bottled water. *Radio New Zealand*. Retrieved from https://tinyurl.com/y7zm8g6j

Duncan, C. (2019, December 29). Indian police officer tells citizenship law protesters to go to Pakistan as death till rises. *The Independent*. Retrieved from https://tinyurl.com/y7hwyzky

Dutta, M. (2011). *Communicating social change: Structure, culture, and agency*. New York: Routledge.

Dutta, M. (2012). *Voices of resistance: Communication and social change*. West Lafayette, IN: Purdue University Press.

Dutta, M. (2014, August 24). *(In)Civility and Phyllis Wise: When claims to academic freedom ring hollow. Culture-centred approach blog*. Retrieved from https://tinyurl.com/yastskyc

Dutta, M., & Pal, M. (2011). Public relations and marginalization in a global context: A postcolonial critique. In N. Bardhan & C. K. Weaver (Eds.), *Public relations in global cultural contexts: Multiparadigmatic perspectives* (pp. 195–225). New York: Routledge.

Dutta, M. J., & Pal, M. (2010). Dialog theory in marginalized settings: A subaltern studies approach. *Communication Theory, 20*, 363–386.

Dutta-Bergman, M. (2005). Civil society and public relations: Not so civil after all. *Journal of Public Relations Research, 17*(3), 267–289.

Dwinell, A., & Olivera, M. (2014). The water is ours damn it! Water commoning in Bolivia. *Community Development Journal, 49*(S1), 44–52.

Edwards, L. (2011). Defining the 'object' of public relations research: A new starting point. *Public Relations Inquiry, 1*(1), 7–30.

Edwards, L. (2012). Defining the 'object' of public relations research: A new starting point. *Public Relations Inquiry, 1*(1), 7–30.

Edwards, L. (2014). *Power, diversity and public relations*. London: Routledge.

Edwards, L. (2016). The role of public relations in deliberative systems. *Journal of Communication, 66*, 60–81.

Edwards, L. (2018). *Understanding public relations: Theory, culture, society*. London: Sage.

Edwards, L., & Hodges, C. (2011). Introduction: Implications of a (radical) socio-cultural 'turn' in public relations scholarship. In L. Edwards & C. Hodges (Eds.), *Public relations, society and culture: Theoretical and empirical explorations* (pp. 1–14). New York: Routledge.

Edwards, L., Ihlen, O., & Somerville, I. (Eds.). (2019). *Public relations and society: The generative power of history.* London: Routledge.

Elbein, S. (2017, January 31). The youth group that launched a movement at standing rock. *The New York Times.* Retrieved from https://tinyurl.com/gsp9exr

Elkington, J. (1994). Towards the sustainable corporation: Win-win-win business strategies for sustainable development. *California Management Review, 36,* 90–100.

Estes, N. (2016, September 18). Fighting for our lives: #NoDAPL in historical context. *Red Nation.* Retrieved from https://tinyurl.com/h8eurvs

Etchart, L. (2017). The role of indigenous peoples in combating climate change. *Palgrave Communications, 3,* 17085. https://doi.org/10.1057/palcomms.2017.85

Farooqi, I. (2020). Citizenship as participation: Muslim women protestors of Shaheen Bagh. *Economic and Political Weekly, LV*(4), 13–15.

Finley-Brook, M. (2014). Climate justice advocacy. *Public Diplomacy Magazine, 12,* 11–15.

Fisk, R. (2005). *The great war of civilization: The conquest of the middle east.* New York: Harper Collins.

Flanagan, R. (2020, January 3). Australia is committing climate suicide. *New York Times.* Retrieved from www.nytimes.com/2020/01/03/opinion/australia-fires-climate-change.html

Fletcher, C., van Heelsum, A., & Roggeband, C. (2018). Water privatization, hegemony and civil society: What motivates individuals to protest about water privatization? *Journal of Civil Society, 14*(3), 241–256.

Foran, J., & Widick, R. (2013). Breaking barriers to climate justice. *Contexts, 12*(2), 34–39.

Forty Second Amendment to the Constitution of India. (1976). Retrieved from https://tinyurl.com/y8cex87f

Foucault, M. (1980). *Power/knowledge.* New York: Pantheon.

Fraser, N. (1986). Toward a discourse ethic of solidarity. *Praxis International, 5*(4), 425–429.

Fraser, N. (2007). Transnationalizing the public sphere: On the legitimacy and efficacy of public opinion in a post-Westphalian world. *Theory Culture & Society, 24*(4), 7–30.

Gaard, G. (2015). Ecofeminism and climate change. *Women's Studies International Forum, 49,* 20–33.

Gaur, V. (2019, December 15). After Jamia, police uses brute force to quell protests at AMU. *The Economic Times.* Retrieved from https://tinyurl.com/yaxknmsp

Gayle, G. (2020, February 7). Climate activists bring Trojan Horse to British Museum in BP protest. *The Guardian.* Retrieved from https://tinyurl.com/y79nffrw

Ghosh, A. (2008). *A sea of poppies.* London: John Murray.

Ghosh, A. (2016). *The great derangement.* Chicago: University of Chicago Press.

Girvan, A. (2017). Trickster carbon: Stories, science, and postcolonial interventions for climate justice. *Journal of Political Ecology, 24*(1), 1038–1054.

Global Alliance Against REDD+ (2016, May 18). *Indigenous peoples denounce carbon offsets at United Nations.* Demand Cancellation of REDD+. Retrieved from https://tinyurl.com/ybff2fdp

Goldberg, M. (2018, December 7). Anti-Zionism isn't the same as anti-Semitism. *New York Times.* Retrieved from https://tinyurl.com/y96l5w7b

Grace, P. (1986). *Potiki.* Auckland: Viking.

Gramsci, A. (1971). *Selections from the prison notebooks.* New York: International Publishers.

Gray, J. (2009). *False dawn: The delusions of global capitalism.* London: Granta.

Grunig, J. (1989). Sierra club study shows who become activists. *Public Relations Review, 15*(3), 3–24.

Grunig, J. (Ed.). (1992). *Excellence in public relations and communication management.* Hillsdale, NJ: Lawrence Erlbaum.

Grunig, J., & Hunt, T. (1984). *Managing public relations.* New York: Holt, Rinehart and Winston.

Grunig, L. A., Grunig, J. E., & Dozier, D. M. (2002). *Excellent public relations and effective organizations: A study of communication management in three Countries.* Mahwah, NJ: Lawrence Erlbaum.

Guha, R. (1982). *Subaltern studies I.* New Delhi: Oxford University Press.

Guha, R. (1983). *Elementary aspects of peasant insurgency in colonial India.* New Delhi: Oxford University Press.

Guha, R. (2001). Subaltern studies: Projects of our time and their convergence. In I. Rodriguez (Ed.), *The Latin American subaltern studies reader* (pp. 35–46). Durham, NC: Duke University Press.

Gwynn, S. (2019, January 21). BP launches biggest global campaign in a decade. *Campaign.* Retrieved from https://tinyurl.com/y8kokbjq

Haggard, H. R. (1885/2007). *King Solomon's mines.* London: Penguin.

Hallward, M. C. (2013). *Transnational activism and the Israeli-Palestinian conflict.* New York, NY: Palgrave Macmillan.

Haraway, D., Ishikawa, N., Gilbert, S. F., Olwig, K., Tsing, A., & Bubandt, N. (2016). Anthropologists are talking about the Anthropocene. *Ethnos, 81,* 535–564.

Hartsock, N. (1983). *Money, sex, and power: Toward a feminist historical materialism.* Boston: Northeastern University Press.

Heath, R. L. (2001). A rhetorical enactment rationale for public relations: The good organization communicating well. In R. L. Heath (Ed.), *Handbook of public relations* (pp. 31–50). Thousand Oaks, CA: Sage.

Heath, R. L. (Ed.). (2010). *The Sage handbook of public relations.* Thousand Oaks, CA: Sage.

Heath, R. L., Toth, E., & Waymer, D. (Eds.). (2009). *Rhetorical and critical approaches to public relations II.* New York: Routledge.

Henty, G. (1884/2017). *By sheer pluck: A tale of the Ashanti war.* Canton, OH: Pinnacle Press.

The Hindu. (2004, January 24). Water is not a private property, says Plachimada declaration. Retrieved from https://tinyurl.com/y8h23awo

Hjerm, M., & Bohman, A. (2014). Is it getting worse? Anti-immigrants attitudes in Europe during the 21th century. In C. Sandelind (Ed.), *European populism and winning the immigration debate* (pp. 41–64). Brussels: European Liberal Forum.

Hoggan, J., & Littlemore, R. (2010). *Climate cover-up: The crusade to deny global warming*. Berkeley: Greystone Books.

Holden, E. (2020, January 8). How the oil industry has spent billions to control the climate change conversation. *The Guardian*. Retrieved from https://tinyurl.com/yf2sjjn3

Holmstrom, N. (2018). The dialectic of the individual and the collective: An ecological imperative. *Radical Philosophy Review, 21*(1), 77–101.

Holtzhausen, D. R. (2014). *Public relations as activism: Postmodern approaches to theory and practice*. New York: Routledge.

Human Rights Watch. (2019, April 23). *US: States use anti-boycott laws to punish responsible businesses*. Retrieved from https://tinyurl.com/y22tpgep

Hutton, J., Goodman, M., Alexander, J., & Genest, C. (2001). Reputation management: The new face of corporate public relations? *Public Relations Review, 27*(3), 247–261.

IATP (Institute for Agriculture and Trade Policy). (2002). IMF and World Bank push water privatization and full cost recovery on poor countries. In *News and notices for IMF and World Bank watchers*. Minneapolis, MN. Retrieved from https://tinyurl.com/ycaywjmx

Ihlen, Ø. (2008). Mapping the environment of corporate social responsibility: Stakeholders, publics, and the public sphere. *Corporate Communications, 13*(2), 135–146.

Ihlen, Ø., & Heath, R. L. (2018). *Handbook of organizational rhetoric and communication*. Chichester, UK: Wiley-Blackwell.

Ihlen, Ø., van Ruler, B., & Frederiksson, M. (Eds.). (2009). *Public relations and social theory*. New York: Routledge.

IISD (International Institute for Sustainable Development). (2001, October 29, November 9). *Linkages: Seventh conference of the parties to the UN framework convention on climate change*. Marrakesh, Morocco. Retrieved from https://tinyurl.com/y7boeydq

Indigenous Environmental Network (IEN). (n.d). Website. Retrieved from www.ienearth.org/

International Bottled Water Association (IBWA). (2017, March 9). Bottled water – The nation's healthiest packaged beverage is officially America's favorite. *Media Release*. Retrieved from https://tinyurl.com/ycpkjfdo

IBWA (n.d.) International Bottled Water Association website. Retrieved from https://www.bottledwater.org/

Jacob, J. (2020, January 25). Election body asks police to file FIR against BJP's Kapil Mishra for communal tweet. *NDTV*. Retrieved from https://tinyurl.com/yd38k6lp

Jaffee, D., & Case, R. (2018). Draining us dry: Scarcity discourses in contention over bottled water extraction. *Local Environment, 23*(4), 485–501.

Jain, K. (2019, May 3). Cow vigilantes and the rise of Hindu nationalism. *Kennedy School Review*. Retrieved from https://tinyurl.com/y97mo65n

Jefferess, D. (2008). *Postcolonial resistance: Culture, liberation, and transformation*. Toronto: University of Toronto Press.

Johnson, B. (2020, January 20). *PM Africa investment summit speech*. Retrieved from https://tinyurl.com/yd3v583y

Joy, S. (2019, November 20). NRC will be carried out across India: Amit Shah in RS. *Deccan Herald*. Retrieved from https://tinyurl.com/ybh4e26a

Kaplan, S. (2019, September 25). Teen girls are leading the climate strikes and helping change the face of environmentalism. *Washington Post*. Retrieved from https://tinyurl.com/y3eekkbj

Keough, S. B., & Youngstedt, S. M. (2018). 'Pure water' in Niamey, Niger: The backstory of sachet water in a landscape of waste. *Africa, 88*, 38–62.

Khan, A. M. (2003). Persecution of the Ahmadiyya community in Pakistan: An analysis under international law and international relations. *Harvard Human Rights Journal, 16*, 217–244.

Kincaid, J. (1988). *A small place*. New York: Farrar, Straus, Giroux.

Klein, N. (2014). *This changes everything: Capitalism vs. the climate*. New York: Simon & Schuster.

Knight, B. (2019, November 6). Amitav Ghosh: What the west doesn't get about the climate crisis. *Deustsche Welle*. Retrieved from https://tinyurl.com/udxa4wt

Kuchay, B. (2019, December 25). Student's hand amputated as violence grips citizenship protests. *Al Jazeera*. Retrieved from https://tinyurl.com/wpezogl

Kurian, A. (2020, February 25). Indian women protest new citizenship laws, joining a global 'fourth wave' feminist movement. *The Conversation*. Retrieved from https://tinyurl.com/y8ga5g45

Kurian, P. (2000). *Engendering the environment? Gender in the World Bank's environmental policies*. Aldershot: Ashgate.

Kurian, P. (2017). Feminist futures in the Anthropocene: Sustainable citizenship and the challenges of climate change and social justice. *Women's Studies Journal, 31*(1), 104–107.

Kurian, P., Munshi, D., & Bartlett, R. V. (2014). Sustainable citizenship for a technological world: Negotiating deliberative dialectics. *Citizenship Studies, 18*(3–4), 393–409.

Larson, A. M., Solisa, D., Duchelle, A. E., Atmadja, S., Resosudarmo, I. A. P., Dokken, T., & Komalasari, M. (2018). Gender lessons for climate initiatives: A comparative study of REDD+ impacts on subjective wellbeing. *World Development, 108*, 86–102.

Laville, S. (2019, December 4). Lawyers lodge complaint over BP's 'misleading' ad campaign. *The Guardian*. Retrieved from https://tinyurl.com/ya2qfxxb

Leahy, S. (2013, November 26). Young and restless: Canadian youth dismayed at Canada's climate performance. *The Narwhal*. Retrieved from https://tinyurl.com/ya329pql

Ledford, H. (2016). Trump's immigration stance stokes fears for science. *Nature, 532*(7597).

Leitch, S., & Motion, J. (2010). Publics and public relations: Effecting change. In R. Heath (Ed.), *The Sage handbook of public relations* (pp. 99–110). Thousand Oaks, CA: Sage.

Leonard, A. (2010). *The story of water. Video produced by the story of stuff project and free range studios.* Retrieved from www.youtube.com/watch?v=Se12y9hSOM0

L'Etang, J. (2005). Critical public relations: Some reflections. *Public Relations Review, 31,* 521–526.

L'Etang, J. (2016). Public relations, activism and social movements: Critical perspectives. *Public Relations Inquiry, 5*(3), 207–2011.

L'Etang, J., McKie, D., Snow, N., & Xifra, J. (Eds.). (2016). *The Routledge handbook of critical public relations.* London: Routledge.

L'Etang, J., & Pieczka, M. (Eds.). (2006). *Public relations: Critical debates and contemporary practice.* Mahwah, NJ: Lawrence Erlbaum Associates.

Lopez, O., & Jacobs, A. (2018, July 14). In town with little water, Coca-Cola is everywhere. So is diabetes. *The New York Times.* Retrieved from https://tinyurl.com/yaqwe9v6

Ludden, D. (Ed.). (1996). *Making India Hindu: Religion, community, and the politics of democracy in India.* New Delhi: Oxford University Press.

MacGregor, S. (2019). Zooming in, calling out: (M)anthropogenic climate change through the lens of gender. In K.-K. Bhavnani, J. Foran, P. Kurian, & D. Munshi (Eds.), *Climate futures: Reimagining global climate justice* (pp. 57–63). London: Zed Books.

Mackey, E. (1998). Becoming indigenous: Land, belonging, and the appropriation of aboriginality in Canadian nationalist narratives. *Social Analysis, 42*(2), 150–178.

MacLennan, C. (2020, March 5). Bottled water has reached its tipping point. The time for a moratorium is now. *The Spinoff.* Retrieved from https://tinyurl.com/y7e6cm3x

Macqueen, D. (2013). *Gender and REDD+. IIED (International Institute for Environment and Development).* Retrieved from www.iied.org/gender-redd

Maloney, J. (2019, June 21). Coke and Pepsi want to sell you bottled water without the bottle. *Wall Street Journal.* Retrieved from https://tinyurl.com/yctkytjz

Mander, H. (2019, December 11). If parliament passes the citizenship amendment bill, India's constitutional structure, as we know it, will lose its soul. *The Indian Express.* Retrieved from https://tinyurl.com/y7ctghey

Mankekar, P. (2015). *Unsettling India: Affect, temporality, transnationality.* Durham, NC: Duke University Press.

MarketWatch. (2019, September 12). Bottled water market size, share | Industry report, 2026. Press Release. Retrieved from https://tinyurl.com/y78c2dou

Marlow, I. (2019, February 20). Cow vigilantes in India killed at least 44 people, report finds. *Bloomberg.* Retrieved from https://tinyurl.com/y8z6pk5e

Marquis, C., Toffel, M., & Zhou, Y. (2016). Scrutiny, norms, and selective disclosure: A global study of greenwashing. *Organization Science, 27*(2), 483–504.

Martin, J. N., & Nakayama, T. K. (1999). Thinking dialectically about culture and communication. *Communication Theory, 9*(1), 1–25.

Martin, J. N., & Nakayama, T. K. (2010). *Intercultural communication in contexts* (5th ed.). Boston, MA: McGraw-Hill.

Martínez-Alier, J. (2003). *The environmentalism of the poor: A study of ecological conflicts and valuation.* Cheltenham, UK: Edward Elgar.

Mathur, S. (2019, December 18). Jamia students scarred by the violence on campus. *The Hindu Business Line.* Retrieved from https://tinyurl.com/ycx248x6

McClintock, A. (1995). *Imperial leather.* London: Routledge.

McKie, D., & Munshi, D. (2007). *Reconfiguring public relations: Ecology, equity and enterprise.* London: Routledge.

McMahon, S. F. (2014). The boycott, divestment, sanctions campaign: Contradictions and challenges. *Race & Class, 55*(4), 65–81.

McNulty, J. (2008, April 8). Shopping our way to safety: Sociology professor Andrew Szasz says 'buying green' may be lulling consumers into a false sense of security. *UCSC News.* Retrieved from https://news.ucsc.edu/2008/04/2098.html

Mearsheimer, J. J., & Walt, S. M. (2007). *The Israel Lobby and U.S. Foreign policy.* New York, NY: Farrar, Strauss, and Giroux.

Mickey, T. J. (2003). *Deconstructing public relations: Public relations criticism.* Mahwah, NJ: Lawrence Erlbaum.

Milne, S., Mahanty, S., To, P., Dresslerb, W., Kanowski, P., & Thavat, M. (2019). Learning from 'actually existing' REDD+: A synthesis of ethnographic findings. *Conservation and Society, 17*(1), 84–95.

Misiedjan, D., & Gupta, J. (2014). Indigenous communities: Analyzing their right to water under different international legal regimes. *Utrecht Law Review, 10*(2), 77–90.

Mitchell, D. (2002). Cultural landscapes: The dialectical landscape – Recent landscape research in human geography. *Progress in Human Geography, 26,* 381–389.

Molina, L. (2016, November 4). *How Greenpeace is showing up as an ally in the Dakota access pipeline fight. Greenpeace US.* Retrieved from https://tinyurl.com/y8rezscl

Moloney, K. (2006). *Rethinking public relations: Propaganda and democracy.* London: Routledge.

Moloney, K., & McGrath, C. (2020). *Rethinking public relations: Persuasion, democracy, and society.* London: Routledge.

Moloney, K., & McKie, D. (2016). Changes to be encouraged: Radical turns in PR theorisation and small-step evolutions in PR practice. In J. L'Etang, D. McKie, N. Snow, & J. Xifra (Eds.), *The Routledge handbook of critical public relations* (pp. 151–161). New York: Routledge.

Monbiot, G. (2019, June 26). Shell is not a green saviour. *The Guardian.* Retrieved from https://tinyurl.com/y5pp2jjq

Monbiot, G. (2020, March 18). Our politics isn't designed to protect the public from Covid-19. *The Guardian.* Retrieved from https://tinyurl.com/typbw7l

Motion, J., & Letich, S. (1996). A discursive perspective from New Zealand: Another world view. *Public Relations Review, 22*(3), 297–309.

Motion, J., & Leitch, S. (2016). Critical discourse analysis: A search for meaning and power. In J. L'Etang, D. McKie, N. Snow, & J. Xifra (Eds.), *The Routledge handbook of critical public relations* (pp. 142–150). New York: Routledge.

Mules, P. (2019). Changing representations of activists and activism in public relations textbooks. *Journal of Communication Management, 23*(1), 18–30.

Mulvey, K., Allen, M., & Fromhoff, P. C. (2019, December 17). Fossil fuel companies claim they're helping fight climate change: The reality is different. *Bulletin of the Atomic Scientists.* Retrieved from https://tinyurl.com/u55kx8z

Munnayer, Y. (2014, July 10). How BDS is educating the public about Israel's brutal policies. *The Nation*. Retrieved from https://tinyurl.com/pprw5ze

Munshi, D., Broadfoot, K., & Hall, M. (2017). Postcolonial approaches. In C. R. Scott & L. Lewis (Eds.), *The international encyclopedia of organizational communication* (pp. 1886–1896). Hoboken, NJ: Wiley-Blackwell.

Munshi, D., & Edwards, L. (2011). Understanding 'race' in/and public relations: Where do we start and where should we go? *Journal of Public Relations Research, 23*(4), 349–367.

Munshi, D., & Kurian, P. (2005). Imperializing spin cycles: A postcolonial look at public relations, greenwashing, and the separation of publics. *Public Relations Review, 31*(4), 513–520.

Munshi, D., & Kurian, P. (2007). The case of the subaltern public: A postcolonial investigation of CSR's (o)missions. In S. May, G. Cheney, & J. Roper (Eds.), *The debate over corporate social responsibility* (pp. 438–447). New York: Oxford University Press.

Munshi, D., & Kurian, P. (2015). Imagining organizational communication as sustainable citizenship. *Management Communication Quarterly, 29*(1), 153–159.

Munshi, D., & Kurian, P. (2016). Public relations and sustainable citizenship: Towards a goal of representing the unrepresented. In J. L'Etang, D. McKie, N. Snow, & J. Xifra (Eds.), *The Routledge handbook of critical public relations* (pp. 405–414). New York: Routledge.

Munshi, D., & Kurian, P. (2020). *Problematizing promotional cultures: Disrupting hierarchies and hegemonies towards sustainable citizenship*. Keynote address at the European Communication Research and Education Association (ECREA) conference on Complexity, hybridity, liminality: Challenges of researching contemporary promotional cultures. London School of Economics February 21.

Munshi, D., Kurian, P., Foran, J., & Bhavnani, K.-K. (2019). The future is ours to seek: Changing the inevitability of climate chaos to prospects of hope and justice. In K.-K. Bhavnani, J. Foran, P. Kurian, & D. Munshi (Eds.), *Climate futures: Reimagining global climate justice* (pp. 1–8). London: Zed Books.

Munshi, D., Kurian, P., & Xifra, J. (2017). An (other) 'story' in history: Challenging colonialist public relations in novels of resistance. *Public Relations Review, 43*(2), 366–374.

Munshi, D., & Pal, M. (2018). Colonialism/Post-colonialism. In R. L. Heath & W. Johansen (Eds.), *The international encyclopedia of strategic communication*. Hoboken, NJ: Wiley.

Narain, S. (2009, January 1). A million mutinies. *New Internationalist*. Retrieved from https://newint.org/features/2009/01/01/climate-justice-resistance

Narain, S. (2019, December 19). Climate emergency CoP 25: Circumventing climate action. *Down to Earth*. Retrieved from https://tinyurl.com/yanpvcyq

Nestle (2017). Company website. Retrieved from https://www.nestlepurelife.com/ca/en-ca

New Zealand Law Society. (2019). *Waitangi tribunal freshwater report released*. Retrieved from https://tinyurl.com/y7g4t7r6

Ninawa Huni Kui. (2014). Brazilian indigenous leader: Carbon trading scheme "REDD" a false solution to climate change. *Democracy Now*. Retrieved from https://tinyurl.com/ldnktpj

Noisecat,J.B.(2016,November24).TheIndigenousrevolution.*Jacobin*.Retrievedfrom www.jacobinmag.com/2016/11/standing-rock-dakota-access-pipeline-obama/

O'Brien, K., Selboe, E., & Hayward, B. (2018). Exploring youth activism on climate change: Dutiful, disruptive, and dangerous dissent. *Ecology and Society, 23*(3), 42.

Olivera, O. (2004). *Cochabamba! Water rebellion in Bolivia* (T. Lewis, Trans.). Cambridge, MA: South End Press.

Orange, C. (1987/2010). *The treaty of Waitangi*. Wellington: Bridget Williams Books.

Oreskes, N. (2004). The scientific consensus on climate change. *Science 306*(5702), 1686.

Oreskes, N., & Conway, E. M. (2011). *Merchants of doubt: How a handful of scientists obscured the truth on issues from tobacco smoke to global warming*. New York: Bloomsbury Publishing USA.

Ortiz, G. (2011, March 21). Latin America: Wave of water privatisation over; coverage challenge remains. *Inter Press Service News Agency*. Retrieved from https://tinyurl.com/yahsl7rz

Ott, H., Sterk, W., & Watanabe, R. (2008). The Bali roadmap: New horizons for global climate policy. *Climate Policy, 8*, 91–95.

Pacheco-Vega, R. (2019). (Re)theorizing the politics of bottled water: Water insecurity in the context of weak regulatory regimes. *Water, 11*, 658.

Pearce, F. (2017). *In Honduras, defending nature is a deadly business*. Retrieved from https://tinyurl.com/yblzt2rk

Peirsson-Hagger, E. (2019, July 20). Can we decolonise the British Museum? *New Statesman*. Retrieved from https://tinyurl.com/yyhu3ux8

Peled, M. (n.d.). Tear down the wall. *Miko Peled's blog*. Retrieved from http://mikopeled.com/

Peled, M. (2013). *The general's son: Journey of an Israeli in Palestine*. Charlottesville, VA: Just World Books.

Petronzio, M. (2016, December 6). *How young Native Americans built and sustained the #NoDAPL movement*. Mashable. Retrieved from https://tinyurl.com/y9d2d5qs

Piketty, T. (2014). *Capital in the 21st century*. Cambridge, MA: Harvard University Press.

Pogrund, B. (2015, May 22). Israel has many injustices. But it is not an apartheid state. *The Guardian*. Retrieved from https://tinyurl.com/ycf5edv6

Press Information Bureau. (2019). *Parliament passes the citizenship (Amendment) bill 2019*. Retrieved from https://pib.gov.in/newsite/PrintRelease.aspx?relid=195783

Privott, M. (2019). An ethos of responsibility and indigenous women water protectors in the #NoDAPL movement. *American Indian Quarterly, 43*(1), 74–99.

Proulx, G., & Crane, N. J. (2020). "To see things in an objective light": The Dakota access pipeline and the ongoing construction of settler colonial landscapes. *Journal of Cultural Geography, 37*(1), 46–66.

PTI (Press Trust of India). (2010, April 26). BASIC group wants global deal on climate change by 2011. *The Hindu*. Retrieved from https://tinyurl.com/yblfmad4

PTI (Press Trust of India). (2019, December 26). Cop action worse than colonial record: Habib. *The Telegraph*. Retrieved from https://tinyurl.com/y95v34eu

PTI (Press Trust of India). (2020a, January 22). India fulfilled its 'moral duty' by Enacting CAA, says Defence Minister Rajnath Singh. *News18*. Retrieved from https://tinyurl.com/vj8ylty

PTI (Press Trust of India). (2020b, January 2). Protest against Pakistan's atrocities on minorities, Modi tells anti-CAA protesters. *The Economic Times*. Retrieved from https://tinyurl.com/ya33mpxy

PTI (Press Trust of India). (2020c, January 17). National anthem is a protest song: TM Krishna. *Deccan Herald*. Retrieved from https://tinyurl.com/yb8s7dys

Pulido, L. (2016). Flint, environmental racism, and racial capitalism. *Capitalism Nature Socialism, 27*(3), 1–16.

Radio New Zealand. (2017, February 2). *Tests reveal source of Havelock North water contamination*. Retrieved from https://tinyurl.com/yauzwcn3

Radio New Zealand. (2020, January 14). *Māori water rights case aims to stop water bottlers*. Retrieved from https://tinyurl.com/ycb87p4t

Ranganathan, M. (2016). Thinking with Flint: Racial liberalism and the roots of an American water tragedy. *Capitalism Nature Socialism, 27*(3), 17–33.

Rapid Transition Alliance. (2019, January 28). *Turning the tide of water privatization – The rise of the new municipal movement*. Retrieved from https://tinyurl.com/yxxwrmk8

Redden, E. (2015, December 1). Another association backs Israel boycott. *Inside Higher Ed*. Retrieved from https://tinyurl.com/yb8q7ojy

Rhys, J. (1966). *Wide Sargasso Sea*. New York: W.W. Norton & Co.

Ritter, K. (2019, June 28). 2.2 billion people still don't have access to clean drinking water. *World Economic Forum*. Retrieved from https://tinyurl.com/yxzfhzu3

Robb, E. (2019). *#youthwashing: The fossil fuel industries' latest marketing tool. UK Youth climate coalition*. Retrieved from https://tinyurl.com/yaru7etb

Roberts, J. T., & Parks, B. C. (2009). Ecologically unequal exchange, ecological debt, and climate justice: The history and implications of three related ideas for a new social movement. *International Journal of Comparative Sociology, 50*(3–4), 385–409.

Roy, A. (2004). *An ordinary person's guide to empire*. Boston, MA: South End Press.

Said, E. (1978). *Orientalism*. New York: Pantheon.

Said, E. (2003). *Culture and resistance: Conversations with Edward Said* (D. Barsamian, Ed.). Boston, MA: South End Press.

Sampathkumar, M. (2019, December 3). Thunberg isn't the only young voice we should be listening to. *The New Republic*. Retrieved from https://tinyurl.com/y7fbfhq5

Saran, M. (2020, January 26). Putting the 'public' back in 'Republic.' *Deccan Herald*. Retrieved from https://tinyurl.com/y7t4r9rp

Schultz, K. (2019, December 22). Modi defends Indian citizenship law amid violent protests. *New York Times*. Retrieved from https://tinyurl.com/y9ozcm47

Seymour, F. (n.d.). Looking back; looking forward: REDD+. *Nature4Climate*. Retrieved from https://tinyurl.com/y77sprbn

Sharoni, S. (2012). Gender and conflict transformation in Israel/Palestine. *Journal of International Women's Studies*, *13*(4), 113–128.

Shell (2019, April 8). Shell invests in nature as part of broad drive to tackle CO_2 emissions. *Shell Media Release*. Retrieved from https://tinyurl.com/y9q4wpfh

Shimo, A. (2018, October 4). While Nestlé extracts millions of litres from their land, residents have no drinking water. *The Guardian*. Retrieved from https://tinyurl.com/y4ps5con

Shiva, V. (2002). *Water wars: Privatization, pollution, and profit*. Boston: South End Press.

Smith, L. T. (1999/2012). *Decolonizing methodologies: Research and indigenous peoples*. London: Zed.

Snehi, Y. (2003). Hindutva as an ideology of cultural nationalism. *Social Change*, *33*(4), 10–24.

Sommerfeldt, E., Kent, M., & Taylor, M. (2012). Activist practitioner perspectives of website public relations: Why aren't activist websites fulfilling the dialogic promise? *Public Relations Review*, *38*, 303–312.

Steinman, E. (2019). Why was Standing Rock and the #NoDAPL campaign so historic? Factors affecting American Indian participation in social movement collaborations and coalitions. *Ethnic and Racial Studies*, *42*(7), 1070–1090.

Stevenson, R. L. (1882/2001). *Treasure Island*. London: Electric Book Company.

Stiglitz, J. (2002). *Globalization and its discontents*. New York: W.W. Norton & Co.

Sturgeon, N. (1997). *Ecofeminist natures: Race, gender, feminist theory and political action*. New York: Routledge.

Subramaniam, M. (2019, May 21). Anthropocene now: Influential panel votes to recognize Earth's new epoch. *Nature*. Retrieved from www.nature.com/articles/d41586-019-01641-5

Sultana, F. (2018). Water justice: Why it matters and how to achieve it. *Water International*, *43*(4), 483–493.

Sultana, F., Mohanty, C. T., & Miraglia, S. (2013). *Gender, justice and public water for all: Insights from Dhaka, Bangladesh*. Occasional Paper No. 18. Municipal Services Project. Retrieved from https://tinyurl.com/y98p54hs

Supran, G., & Oreskes, N. (2020, January 20). Big oil is the new big tobacco: Congress must use its power to investigate. *The Guardian*. Retrieved from https://tinyurl.com/yb4nzhvo

Szasz, A. (2007). *Shopping Our way to safety: How we changed from protecting the environment to protecting ourselves*. Minneapolis: University of Minnesota Press.

Talbot, I., & Singh, G. (2009). *The partition of India*. Cambridge, UK: Cambridge University Press.

Taskin, B. (2020, January 28). The 8-yr-old Manipuri climate change activist who doesn't want to be called 'India's Greta.' *The Print*. Retrieved from https://tinyurl.com/t542kms

Thapar, R. (1989). Imagined religious communities? Ancient history and the modern search for a Hindu identity. *Modern Asian Studies, 23*(2), 209–231.

Thrall, N. (2018, August 14). BDS: How a controversial non-violent movement has transformed the Israeli-Palestinian debate. *The Guardian.* Retrieved from https://tinyurl.com/yaup4ubt

Thunberg, G. (2019, March 15). Think we should be at school? Today's climate strike is the biggest lesson of all. *The Guardian.* Retrieved from https://tinyurl.com/y4k5ndrl

Thunberg, G. (2020, February 28). *Speech at College Green.* Bristol, UK.

Tierney, K. (2008). Hurricane Katrina: Catastrophic impacts and alarming lessons. In J. Quigley & L. Rosenthal (Eds.), *Risking house and home: Disasters, cities and public policy* (pp. 119–136). Berkeley, CA: Berkeley Public Policy Press.

Times of India (2019, December 30). PM Narendra Modi launches social media campaign in support of CAA. Retrieved from https://tinyurl.com/y7eezvdv

Todd, M. (2019, June 10). Extinction rebellion's tactics are working: It has pierced the bubble of denial. *The Guardian.* Retrieved from https://tinyurl.com/y4rfm3gz

Toledano, M. (2016). Advocating for reconciliation: Public relations, activism, advocacy and dialogue. *Public Relations Inquiry, 5*(3), 277–294.

Toledano, M. (2018). Dialogue, strategic communication, and ethical public relations: Lessons from Martin Buber's political activism. *Public Relations Review, 44*(1), 131–141.

Toledano, M., & McKie, D. (2013). *Public relations and nation building: Influencing Israel.* London: Routledge.

Tutu, D. (2011). Review of *Barghouti, O. Boycott, divestment, sanctions: The global struggle for Palestinian rights.* Chicago, IL: Haymarket Books, Publisher's webpage.

UNESCO (World Water Assessment Programme). (2019). *The United Nations world water development report 2019: Leaving no one behind.* Paris: UNESCO.

UNICEF. (2020, March 13). *Fact sheet.* Retrieved from https://tinyurl.com/yx7j73pw

Union of Concerned Scientists. (2007). *Smoke, mirrors & hot air: How Exxonmobil uses big tobacco's tactics to manufacture uncertainty on climate science.* Cambridge, MA: Union of Concerned Scientists.

United Nations Department of Economic and Social Affairs (UNDESA). (2014, May 29). *The human right to water and sanitation.* Retrieved from https://tinyurl.com/y52jxgl6

United Nations Framework Convention on Climate Change (UNFCCC). (n.d.). Decision CP. 13. *Bali Action Plan.* Retrieved from https://tinyurl.com/ccv8rsa

United Nations Framework Convention on Climate Change (UNFCCC) Newsroom. (2014, September 22). *600,000 people march for climate action.* Retrieved from https://tinyurl.com/yc2zn6v4

United Nations Framework Convention on Climate Change (UNFCCC) Secretariat. (n.d.). *United nations framework convention on climate change.* Retrieved from www.unbonn.org/UNFCCC

United Nations Human Rights Office. (2018, September 18). *Myanmar: UN fact-finding mission releases its full account of massive violations by military in Rakhine, Kachin and Shan States.* Retrieved from https://tinyurl.com/y5kceyuv

United Nations Joint Framework Initiative on Children, Youth and Climate Change. (2010). *Youth participation in the UNFCCC negotiation process: The united nations, young people, and climate change.* Retrieved from https://tinyurl.com/y84j9jpc

Vaughan, A. (2019, September 23). Greta Thunberg: You have stolen my childhood with your empty words. *New Scientist.* Retrieved from https://tinyurl.com/y83x42sj

Veracini, L. (2006). *Israel and settler society.* London: Pluto Press.

Vercic, D., & Zerfass, A. (2016). A comparative excellence framework for communication management. *Journal of Communication Management, 20*(4), 270–288.

Vidal, J. (2017, March 1). As water scarcity deepens across Latin America, political instability grows. *The Guardian.* Retrieved from https://tinyurl.com/hmt4d6s

Vidal, J., & Harvey, F. (2013, November 21). Green groups walk out of UN climate talks. *The Guardian.* Retrieved from https://tinyurl.com/y8szl23g

wa Thiong'o, N. (1967). *A grain of wheat.* Portsmouth, NH: Heinemann.

Walsgard, J., & Holter, M. (2018, March 15). Statoil no longer wants 'oil' in its name. *Bloomberg.* Retrieved from https://tinyurl.com/y9b3mel7

Wearden, G. (2020a, January 23). Greta Thunberg clashes with US treasury secretary in Davos. *The Guardian.* Retrieved from https://tinyurl.com/wfqg3a8

Wearden, G. (2020b, January 24). Greta Thunberg: Davos leaders ignored climate activists' demands. *The Guardian.* Retrieved from https://tinyurl.com/ydgwymsg

Wernick, A. (1991). *Promotional culture: Advertising, ideology and symbolic expression.* Thousand Oaks, CA: Sage.

Whitman, D. (2008). 'Stakeholders' and the politics of environmental policymaking. In J. Park, K. Conca, & M. Finger (Eds.), *The crisis of global environmental governance: Towards a new political economy of sustainability.* New York: Routledge.

Whyte, K. P. (2017). The Dakota access pipeline, environmental injustice, and U.S. colonialism. *Red Ink, 19*(1), 154–167.

Whyte, K. P. (2019). Way beyond the lifeboat: An indigenous allegory of climate justice. In K.-K. Bhavnani, J. Foran, P. Kurian, & D. Munshi (Eds.), *Climate futures: Reimagining global climate justice* (pp. 11–20). London: Zed Books.

Williams, R. (1960). *Culture and society 1780–1950.* London: Chatto & Windus.

World Health Organization (WHO). (2019, June 14). *Drinking water.* Retrieved from www.who.int/news-room/fact-sheets/detail/drinking-water

World Health Organization (WHO). (2020, March 18). *Basic protective measures against the coronavirus.* Retrieved from https://tinyurl.com/vr9owsn

Yellowhammer, A. L., & Iron Eyes, T. (2016). *Stop the Dakota access pipeline. Change.org petition.* Retrieved from www.change.org/p/jo-ellen-darcy-stop-the-dakota-access-pipeline

Young, I. M. (1990). *Justice and the politics of difference.* Princeton, NJ: Princeton University Press.

Index

Supreme Court, United States 43
sustainability 7–8, 11–12, 27, 36;
    social 13
sustainable citizenship *see* citizenship
Sustainable Otakiri (Facebook group) 38
Sweden 19, 28
Switzerland 22
symbols 58, 63
Szasz, Andrew 36

Tanzania 26
tar sands 19
taxation 43, 68
"te Kawanatanga katoa" (governance of
    the land) 67
tea tins 49
teach-ins 45; *see also* protest
technocratic managerialism 17, 25
technology 2, 23, 40
television 18
temperature, global *see* climate, change
tenancy, land 63; *see also* land;
    property
territory, occupation of *see* land
Texas 43
textbooks 60
Thailand 30
Thapar, Romila 58
Thatcher, Margaret 40
think-tanks 12, 16, 18
Third World 12, 22–24, 37–38
Thomas, Iokarenhtha 38
Thrall, Nathan 54–55
Thunberg, Greta 19, 28, 30–31
The Times of India (newspaper) 57
tobacco 21; industry 16
toffee 21
Toledano, Margalit 51
Toronto (Ontario) 47
tourism 70
toxic sludge 41
trade associations 18; deficits 43;
    promotion 21
trade unions 30, 41
traditions 11, 63
transgender people 60
translation, of treaties 67
transport 70
Treasure Island (Stevenson) 49

Treasury, United States 22
treaties 39, 42–43; environmental
    17, 24, 29; Treaty of Fort Laramie
    (1851 & 1868) 43; Treaty of
    Waitangi (1840) 39, 41, 67
trees 25, 46, 66; *see also* forest
trolls, internet 60
"Troy: Myth and reality" (exhibition,
    2019–2020) 15
Trump, Donald 58
trust 3
Tutu, Desmond 55
Twitter 20, 45

UK Youth Climate Coalition 20
UK–Africa Investment Summit
    (London, 2020) 21
UN Climate Action Summit (New
    York, 2019) 19
UN Conference on Environment and
    Development (Rio de Janeiro, 1992)
    28–29
UN Framework Convention on Climate
    Change (UNFCCC) 17, 22, 24, 29, 34
United Kingdom 15, 21, 28, 39–40, 70
United Nations 29, 40, 51, 56; General
    Assembly 39–40; Human Rights
    Council 39–40; Permanent Forum
    on Indigenous Issues 26; Resolution
    194 53–54; *see also* Conferences of
    the Parties (COP)
United States 12, 20, 22, 30, 38, 40–43,
    45, 51–54, 58, 66, 69; Native
    Americans 45
universities 53–54, 60–61; London
    School of Economics and Political
    Science (LSE) 70; Waikato 70
uprisings 63
urbanization 37
Uruguay 41
utilities, public 47
Uttar Pradesh 59

vaccines 70
values 1, 16, 63, 66; corporate 10;
    Hindu 58; *see also* ethics
van Heelsum, Anja 42
vases, painted 15
vehicles, electric 20

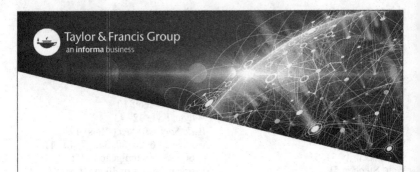

Taylor & Francis Group
an **informa** business

Taylor & Francis eBooks

www.taylorfrancis.com

A single destination for eBooks from Taylor & Francis
with increased functionality and an improved user
experience to meet the needs of our customers.

90,000+ eBooks of award-winning academic content in
Humanities, Social Science, Science, Technology, Engineering,
and Medical written by a global network of editors and authors.

TAYLOR & FRANCIS EBOOKS OFFERS:

A streamlined
experience for
our library
customers

A single point
of discovery
for all of our
eBook content

Improved
search and
discovery of
content at both
book and
chapter level

REQUEST A FREE TRIAL
support@taylorfrancis.com

 Routledge
Taylor & Francis Group

 CRC Press
Taylor & Francis Group

Printed in the United States
by Baker & Taylor Publisher Services

Printed in the United States
by Baker & Taylor Publisher Services